RUNAWAY

HOMELESS

YOUTH

STRENGTHENING SERVICES TO
FAMILIES AND CHILDREN

JACK ROTHMAN

The Center for Child and Family Policy Studies,
School of Social Welfare,
University of California, Los Angeles

Longman
New York & London

Runaway and Homeless Youth: Strengthening Services to Families and Children

Longman, 95 Church Street, White Plains, N.Y. 10601

Associated companies:
Longman Group Ltd., London
Longman Cheshire Pty., Melbourne
Longman Paul Pty., Auckland
Copp Clark Pitman, Toronto

Published in cooperation with the Center for Child and Family
Policy Studies, School of Social Welfare, University of
California, Los Angeles

Senior editor: David J. Estrin
Production editors: Camilla T.K. Palmer and The Bookmakers, Incorporated
Cover design: Susan J. Moore
Production supervisor: Anne Armeny

Library of Congress Cataloging-in-Publication Data

Rothman, Jack.
    Runaway and homeless youth: strengthening services to families
and children / Jack Rothman.
        p.   cm.
    Includes bibliographical references and index.
    ISBN 0-8013-0539-X :
    1. Runaway youth—United States.   2. Homeless youth—United
States.   3. Runaway youth—Services for—United States.   4. Homeless
youth—Services for—United States.   I. Title.
HV1431.R67 1991
362.7′4′0973—dc20   90-6536
                                                                CIP

1 2 3 4 5 6 7 8 9 10-MU-9594939291

To Judy
who helped me to climb the hill
through a great deal of love
and an occasional tug

Contents

Foreword

Nationally televised news programs recently reported a "growing public hostility to the homeless." The discussion revolved mainly around homeless men observed in such public places as doorways, parks, and train stations, and their offensiveness to the public. No mention was made of the critical population of homeless, "throwaway" and runaway children and youth found across the country, in cities and rural areas. One must hope that the reporting omission does not reflect public indifference to the plight of these "discarded" children. A more acceptable explanation is that such youth do not immediately stand out as clearly different from many others of their age. The significant factor is that these adolescents are refugees from an unbearable situation. Homeless or runaway, they have learned ways to avoid detection and have agility in escaping the uncertain consequences of personal attention from a stranger. Fortunately, some new social programs have demonstrated that many of these young people can be helped by persons trained and committed to finding such boys and girls, engaging them, and providing appropriate services.

In this very informative and useful book, Rothman has made a strong case for understanding these youths, viewing them in the context of their families and communities, and proposing services through interagency planning, with critical attention to social policy issues at the levels of family, community, state, and federal government systems.

One of the most notable aspects of Rothman's work here is his comprehensive review of existing empirical research relative to the runaway and homeless adolescent population. The review includes studies of (a) the personal characteristics of these troubled youth, and (b) community programs that serve them and the resultant effects on the underlying problem. Rothman has organized this extensive review in a user-friendly way. A series of major generalizations is offered, centering on (a) typologies of runaways, their reasons for running, self-concepts of runaways, family factors among runaways, and correlates of truancy; and (b) family-oriented intervention, use of volunteers, use of community agency resources, rational intake and disposition processes, use of competent staff, scientifically effective program approaches, and truancy programs. Each generalization is followed by the research findings and the context that support the generalization. Then an "action guideline" for policy and program design is offered. The generalizations, as well as the action guidelines, are suggestive. The intent is to stimulate thought, debate, and new legislation. Even though scientific knowledge about homeless, runaway children is limited, Rothman wants us to consider what is evident, even though it may not yet be clearly corroborated.

Rothman's research synthesis is a marked contribution to thinking about these troubled youth in a scientific context. The supplementary material that is woven in throughout the book—findings from a structured community survey, agency profiles, and the "case in point" that opens each chapter—keeps the reader alert to the components of a holistic system that must be understood if we are to do better in our efforts to help the homeless, runaway youths among us.

Sadly, however, the present organization and delivery of our social services are failing many families and children who desperately require help. Much needed and closely related services are not the responsibility of one system, but are assigned to different systems—child welfare, juvenile justice, health, mental health, schools. Current services are uncoordinated and fragmented. This becomes a major impediment in efforts to help children and youth who have multiple needs, as is characteristic of all homeless, runaway or expelled-from-home adolescents. Child welfare programs are assigned heavy tasks—covering mandated programs with uncertain and insufficient funding and frequently, as well, untrained staff. Add to this the demands of investigating a myriad of abuse reports, and finding homes for children who have experienced fetal abuse or neglect or are infected with AIDS, and it becomes clear why many young people are turned away, discarded and left to the streets. Runaway, homeless, "throwaway" children have experienced chaotic life events and have multiple deprivations. Traditional agencies are typically unprepared to deal with multiple-problem individuals.

A recent report from the Select Committee on Children, Youth, and Families, based on expert testimony as well as on the voices of parents and children, stated that "while there is little doubt that economic and social trends are fueling a collapse in children's services, we found extraordinary failings in these systems that remain within our capacity to control." Repeatedly, witnesses had asked for "a bolder and more sustained redesign and redirection of services for children and families" (Select Committee . . . , 1989, pp. 2–3).

Concern about fragmented services is not new. In the latter part of the nineteenth and early twentieth century, the term "child-saving" was used as an umbrella characterization of social reforms for children. This encompassing designation tended to obscure the co-existence of separate movements on behalf of children. That child-saving was not a single system of reform was noted in 1893 by a committee of the National Conference of Charities and Correction. The committee hoped to bring about an improved degree of conceptual unity among the different child-saving efforts "to the end that the best system will become a more exact science than now." The chairman stated the assumption that "there must be an ideal system, which with modifications to suit conditions, will come to be accepted and adopted generally" (Randall, 1893, p. vi). That ideal system remained elusive. Although drawing from common target populations, the reformers continued to rely upon different philosophies, strategies, and supporting constituencies. Largely unconnected systems of reform for children continued to pursue their separate goals.

This outmoded pattern is still in place, leaving countless children at risk, none more than those children and adolescents who are homeless, runaway, or pushed out of their own homes and unable to fit neatly into the boundaries and services of any one of the existing separate systems—child welfare, mental health, or juvenile justice. Each of these systems continues to maintain artificial distinctions among groups of children and families, ignoring the commonalities among them. Doing so diminishes the chance of a unified organization.

There is another system that bears some responsibility for recognizing the void in services for some of our most vulnerable children and youth—social work education in our colleges and universities. Curricula within various specializations should be reviewed and revised as to the extent to which they help students develop competence for highly intensive, overt family interventions and, as well, knowledge and skill for bringing about new creative programs for young people who can only fare better outside their family situations. In addition, university courses in education, public health, sociology, and psychology should address this population more centrally. Rothman has made a welcomed contribution to an understanding of a most threatened population among our children and youth. His book can inform and inspire all those who are concerned with the need for changes in the social service systems.

Lela B. Costin
Professor Emerita
School of Social Work
University of Illinois at Urbana-Champaign

References

Randall, D.C. 1893. Introduction, *History of child saving in the United States. Report of the Committee on the history of child-saving work*. At the Twentieth National

Conference on Charities and Correction. Chicago, June, 1893. Boston: George H. Ellis.

Select Committee on Children, Youth, and Families, U.S. House of Representatives. 1989. *No place to call home: Discarded children in America*. Washington, D.C.: U.S. Government Printing Office.

Acknowledgments

A phalanx of sponsors, supporters, and assistants contributed materially to the creation and production of this book. This was not one of those books composed by a reclusive scholar closeted in an academic garret. Collective effort and institutional resources played a significant part in facilitating every phase of the undertaking.

Leonard Schneiderman, Dean of the UCLA School of Social Welfare and Director of its Center for Child and Family Policy Studies, was in from the start, providing a special blend of encouragement, wherewithal, and friendship that was critical. The Center's administrative director, Walter Furman, facilitated the work effectively at necessary points.

The Department of Children's Services of Los Angeles County was a cooperative partner in the field study that contributed to this book. It provided community access and legitimation, advice, and monetary aid to propel the endeavor. It was the Department of Children's Services that initially identified runaway and homeless youth as a problem area to be studied. Robert Chaffee, Director of the Department, and Jean McIntosh, then on the policy staff, were instrumental in departmental involvement.

I am grateful to Thomas G. David, who served as director of the UCLA Bush Program in Child Policy Studies, for his aid in conducting the field study in Los Angeles. His widespread contacts in the community had a magical effect in opening doors and enticing participation. Competent and dedicated research assistants made the work pleasurable as well as productive. They are mentioned here, not as a matter of routine formality, but to receive highly merited appreciation. Thanks go out to Jeni Catch, Loring Jones, Frank Ayayla, and Julia Pennbridge. This is an open letter of recommendation for all of them.

A paper by Tom Brock for a doctoral seminar at UCLA helped inform the content of Chapter 5. Tom also graciously consented to the integration of parts of the paper into that chapter.

My colleague Gloria Waldinger provided valuable counsel, drawn from her extensive and intimate knowledge of the field of child welfare. Children's Service Department staff members Stephen Fox and Stacy Savelle participated in a helpful way on the joint University-Department Steering Committee.

Finally, appreciation to Selena Lu-Webster and Laura Rigby for their careful and proficient word-processing contribution that transposed concepts and jottings into finished manuscript pages.

Jack Rothman

Introduction

I wanted to find out from the kids themselves their view of what running away was about. Why did they run, and how did street kids (a pseudonym for homeless) survive? There were five of them at the shelter I visited: two boys and three girls, between fourteen and sixteen years old. The girls spoke up first. The boys, who sat on a couch more at a distance, hung back, apparently feeling the situation out. They must have decided I wasn't there to do them in and eventually joined in also.

The kids made it clear to me that runaways leave home because of *parents*. In many cases the parents are abusive. The abuses, which they described in graphic detail, were physical and sexual and also included psychological "game playing." One of the boys portrayed his father as a violent alcoholic. They said that some parents are extremely restrictive and kids rebel by making a break, often going a little wild with their new freedom. Some kids get kicked out, and others leave on their own, but all are escaping terrible conditions in their homes. After all, one of the girls asked, looking at me intently, "Why would any kid leave a happy environment?"

After you are on your own, the kids said, you try to live with people you think you can trust, like friends, or people you meet on the streets. The people you meet on the streets turn out to be pimps, pushers, or pornographers. Who else is out there waiting and willing to look after you? These leeches are really doing the active outreach work on the streets, not the social work agencies.

Soon after these people take you in, you find yourself hustling or dealing drugs. The girls told of traps they encountered all around them. "Runaways get in these things because they almost always meet the wrong people. These people know you need money, and you fall into their hands." The pimp supplies food, clothing, and shelter and then "really makes you feel like you owe him something." The girls told of a constant atmosphere of danger on the streets. "You can get yourself murdered out there, especially if you try to spring loose from your 'protector.' "

They said that legitimate economic survival on your own is almost impossible, because you can't get a job. In order to receive a work permit, you've got to have a parent's signature, and then you can't get hired because you don't have a high school diploma or a permanent address. So you're on the streets. If you're lucky, you find yourself in a temporary shelter for a couple of weeks. But what then?

EXTENT OF THE PROBLEM

Current research shows a trend toward long-term homelessness for runaway adolescents. This is fueled in part by a pattern of family breakdown, with corresponding rejection, physical abuse, and sexual abuse of young people (McCormack, Janus, and Burgess, 1986; Shane, 1989; Jones, 1988). In one study it was found that some 30 percent of long-term runaways no longer even knew where their parents lived and that 6 percent of even sporadic runaways had lost track of the whereabouts of their parents (Kufeldt and Nimma, 1987). The tendency to assume a pattern of street life is associated with length of time away from the family and distance from home (Kufeldt and Nimmo, 1987). Luna (1987) presents evidence that the lives of these homeless teens are both unstable and hazardous, carrying a heavy emotional penalty.

The incidence of homelessness is exacerbated by the lack of a substantial shelter program, with the United States not matching the provisions of the Homeless Persons Act in Great Britain (Killeen, 1986). Also, many youth who have been under care of the child welfare system are not being adequately prepared for independent living or provided with necessary resources to sustain themselves. Leaving the child welfare system sets the stage for many to enter the ranks of the homeless (Raychaba, 1989). Younger adolescents can be at risk for homeless status even by remaining within the family. This is because in the United States families are the fastest growing population group among homeless people (Edelman and Mihaly, 1989).

Increased teen homelessness may too have been stimulated by greater societal tolerance (or callousness) regarding the homeless condition and way of life. It no longer has the quality of the extremely singular and bizarre phenomenon, together with a sense of shameful deviancy, that it previously projected. It is more acceptable now to choose a homeless life-style for a transitional period of time.

Based on an extensive review of research and scholarship on this subject and a close look at the situation surrounding runaway and homeless adolescents in one American megalopolis, the severity of this problem seems striking. Runaway and homeless teens come from highly disorganized families in varied geographic regions, at all social levels, and, in many cases, their behavior results from past physical or sexual abuse. Fifty percent of the young people we studied did not voluntarily leave home but were pushed out or encouraged to leave by parents. Fewer than half of these youngsters were judged to have realistic prospects of ever returning to their families. Out on the street, they were commonly exploited by pimps, the drug fraternity, and pornographic entrepreneurs. Their health problems were grave. Runaways and homeless youth are unable to care for themselves adequately by obtaining lawful, gainful employment. Research indicates that they exhibit stress and other psychological disabilities far in excess of that experienced by nonrunaways.

Although child abuse is generally perceived as a problem of early childhood, our study uncovered another largely unrecognized abused population —adolescents. However, their plight also involves a form of societal child abuse brought about by ignorance of the problem and failure to act. These hurting teenagers require the kind of community care and concern bestowed on their younger counterparts.

EVOLVING UNDERSTANDING OF THE PROBLEM

In proposing the Runaway Youth Act in 1972 (S2829), the Senate Subcommittee on Juvenile Justice summarized its rationale for federal attention to this problem. Their field investigation found:

1. the number of juveniles who leave and remain away from home without parental permission has increased to alarming proportions, creating a significant law enforcement problem for the communities inundated, and significantly endangering the young people who are without resources and live on the street;
2. that the exact nature of the problem is not well defined because national statistics on the size and profile of the runaway population are not tabulated;
3. that many of these young people, because of their age and situation are urgently in need of temporary shelter and counseling services;
4. that the anxieties and fears of parents whose children have run away from home can best be alleviated by the effective interstate services and the earliest possible contact with their children;
5. that the problem of locating, detaining, and returning runaway children should not be the responsibility of already overburdened police departments and juvenile justice authorities; and

6. that in the view of the interstate nature of the problem, it is the responsibility of the Federal Government to develop accurate reporting of the problem nationally and to develop an effective system of temporary care outside the law enforcement structure. (Runaway Youth Act, 1972)

A bill was enacted by Congress in 1974. It emphasized establishing temporary shelters and instituting a national runaway hotline for contacting parents. Recognizing the limitations of the initial statute in 1977, Congress expanded the program (Juvenile Justice Amendments) to include homeless and raised the sums of grants available to localities. A deepening awareness of the nature of the problem is reflected in 1980 amendments that provided for extension of services specifically to families of homeless youth. Hearings conducted by the House of Representatives in 1983 spotlighted abuse of youth by family members and others as a major additional component of the problem.

Despite the provisions enacted to date, the National Network of Runaway and Youth Services in 1985 decried the inadequacy of resources directed at the problem. Their report made a number of policy recommendations to strengthen the programmatic attack. These included:

- Increase federal funding for the Runaway and Homeless Act in order to provide more shelters.
- Enact of similar legislation at the state level, following the pattern set in New York, Florida, Wisconsin and other jurisdictions.
- Conduct public education/media campaigns setting forth the problems and special needs of these troubled youth.
- Encourage greater coordination and efficiency to providing necessary services, using a National Youth Policy but similar to the Older American Act.

These are potentially productive directions for intervention. However, specific details are missing that give substance to such initiatives. We will endeavor to provide such elaboration, derived from available research evidence and "on the ground" community experience.

PERSPECTIVES

Two viewpoints provide a frame for the analysis that will be presented. One relates to scope of inquiry and the other to attitudes toward helping. A wide range of variables will be examined regarding causes of runaway behavior and modes of intervention to deal with it. Most intervention approaches have had a "blame the victim" quality, in that they assume implicitly that the trouble or disorder is contained within the young person (Leone, 1989). This disregards the contribution of family abuse or disorganization, and social and cultural forces that block or disturb youth development. Leone, Walter, and Wolford (1990) point out that "reliance on any one set of lenses for understanding troublesome behavior fails to inform us fully" (p. 293). They go on to say, consistent with the stance of our analysis, that an examination of this field needs "to include not only traditional person-centered perspectives but also studies of the social environments in which adolescents experience difficulties and the organizational structures and cultural forces associated with our current responses to troubling behavior" (p. 297). We will strive to be appropriately comprehensive in this connection.

The other viewpoint issue concerns the manner in which assistance should be extended to impaired youth.

A perspective on the basic current programmatic approaches to status offenders is suggested by Erickson (1979). He spells out three prevailing philosophies:

- *The "heavy hands" approach:* This assumes that many runaway youth are rebellious, inadequately supervised, "bad kids" who need discipline, toughness, structure, clear expectations, and strong adult models.
- *The "helping hands" approach:* This assumes that runaway youth are often confused, engaged in developmental tasks unnatural for their age, or exposed to harmful parental influences and need psychological counseling, social supports, and direction in their lives.
- *The "hands off" approach:* This assumes that runaway youth are primarily engaged in the experimenting and deviating activities characteristic of adolescence and that intervention programs often are overly punitive or restrictive of the developing adolescent. Therefore, the best policy is to let teenagers alone through a deliberate policy of "radical nonintervention."

This author's personal value system is consistent with the middle, "helping hands" approach, and it would be useful and frank to make this explicit. At the same time, it is true that intervention methods are suited variably to particular youth and situations. Overall, the most fundamental commitment in this book is to knowledge and the scientific enterprise.

The primary resolve is to follow the data wherever they lead, putting aside personal predilections in favor of objective social science results to help shape effective policies and programs for youth.

THE GAP IN THE CURRICULUM

It is ironic and seemingly puzzling that a compelling problem of this magnitude has received so little sustained attention in the social work curriculum and that of other human service professions and social science disciplines. In social work, courses in services to families and children have given scant coverage to the problems and needs of these adolescents, certainly as compared to that lavished on child abuse, adoption, family therapy, and teen pregnancy. The subject of runaways is at the periphery of the field, if, indeed, it is included at all.

There are historical reasons for this, constituting a cultural lag. As will be described in the next chapter, runaways have traditionally been encompassed under the rubric of status offenders, youth whose behavior is designated criminal as a consequence of their age. Truancy is another example of this. For this reason, runaways always were considered part of the criminal justice service system and professional network. When Congress acted to decriminalize status offenders, the courts dropped their traditional responsibility, but no other entity chose to fill the service vacuum left in the community. Runaways have been suspended in a professional no-man's-land. The problems manifested by homeless and runaway youth, and the service provisions needed to address them, indicate that the population assume a more prominent position in the realm of services to families and children. A cultural lag is a normal and understandable phenomenon. When it is accompanied by professional obfuscation, that is not normal or justifiable.

CONTENT AND AUDIENCE

This book is about runaway and homeless adolescents: who they are, how they come to be in limbo, and what kinds of programs and methods exist to deal with their problems. The analysis is a broad-gauged examination of psychological dynamics of individual youth, program features of community service agencies, and policy options aimed at alleviation or prevention of this contemporary social problem.

The volume is designed as a text for a range of courses in human service professional schools and in the social science disciplines. The content will be particularly useful to schools of social work to bolster the curriculum in practice for families and children.

In the field of education, teachers of counseling courses and other curriculum areas focusing on the secondary level will find the research and concepts that are presented to be of value. Sociology courses dealing with social problems, deviancy, and youth issues can be enriched by the immediacy of this subject matter. The areas of clinical and developmental psychology may benefit from the psychosocial approach that is employed, which examines both individual behavior and the social context that can exacerbate personal disability or serve as a positive force for personal growth.

STRUCTURE OF THE BOOK

The book begins with a historical overview (Chapter 1), depicting how runaways and other youthful status offenders have been dealt with over time. Changes in attitudes and legal approaches are delineated.

Chapter 2 comprises a comprehensive review of existing empirical research knowledge, focused on the personal characteristic of the runaway and homeless adolescent population. The potential utility of this information for intervention is brought forward in systematic fashion. The examination of research knowledge is continued in Chapter 3 but with an emphasis on organizational and community programs to service runaways, together with an evaluation of their effects on youth and on the underlying problem condition.

Chapter 4 shifts to an in-depth, graphic portrayal of these issues in a major urban community. Los Angeles has been a national center for the ingathering of detached teens, and the pattern there is both a microcosm of the national scene and a harbinger of things to come. Results of field interviews with knowledgeable, experienced professionals and other community actors, as well as youth themselves, are presented. The manifestations of the problem and the shape of solution strategies as viewed locally are brought to the fore.

Chapter 5 summarizes and integrates the highlights of the presentation, placing it in a systematic policy context. An analytic scheme incorporates multiple system levels in order to provide an encompassing intervention framework.

Case materials are interspersed throughout for purposes of vividly illustrating and personalizing the concepts in human dimension. Their aim is to provide a tone of individuality about runaways to balance the more abstract and substantive content of the chapter. Each chapter begins with a section called "Case in Point," which discusses a professional activity that helps to resolve difficulties of particular young people. The cases describe different types of youth with varied problems. At the end of each chapter there is a "Getting Organized" section, which depicts diverse programs and services of community agencies operating in this field. The agency profiles cover different social contexts, levels, and intervention strategies. These are authentic case materials originating from practitioners and administrators working actively in this field. The cases have been formatted to disguise identities and locales and to preserve confidentially. They have also been edited for ease and clarity of presentation and consistency of voice.

A methodology of intervention design and development (or social research and development) has guided the work of this project (Rothman 1980, 1989). It is described in Appendix A.

Overview: Historical Perspective

(Practitioners Talk About Their Work with Clients)

CAROL

Carol was referred to our shelter at age sixteen by the police. She had been expelled from her home and was requesting a long-term placement. Earlier during her childhood, referrals to local authorities had been made, but the cases had been closed because of "unsubstantiated allegations." On the surface, it seemed like a typical white, working class "incorrigible" teen scenario; she had been truant from school and had been running away and living on the streets for a year. Her mother finally kicked her out, out of desperation, after Carol had threatened to hit her when she tried to regain control. When I met Carol, she said she was tired of this kind of life and wanted a living arrangement where she could go back to school and get her life together.

In a short time, I placed Carol in the foster home where she still lives. The story "under the surface" revealed itself as I kept in touch and got to know her. She was the only child of a mentally ill mother and had been molested by her father during visits by him when she was about seven. She had learned to survive with her irrational mother by developing an angry, overbearing manner, which allowed her to survive at home but didn't help her in relationships with other adults in authority positions. Her defiance and running had been expressions of long held-in anger and hurt over having a mother who baffled and embarrassed her and a father who not only abandoned but molested her. She once told me if only someone had spoken to her as a child and explained to her that her mother had serious problems and it wasn't the fault of either of them, it might have made a difference. She also has told me that if only grown-ups, especially at school, would take the time to ask truant and rebellious kids, "What's wrong? Can I help?" instead of immediately criticizing and punishing, it would help a lot of kids. She said she could not concentrate at school because of troubles at home, and her grades began to fall. She began to skip school. As more time went by, it became harder and harder to return.

When I put Carol into placement, she began the long, difficult task of returning to school after a year's absence and of adjusting herself to a structured family environment. She continued to be rebellious for a while, wanting occasionally to return to her former "hangouts" in "the city." The placement was precarious for about six months. Her anger flared up often, creating crises in the foster family. I spent a great deal of time with her and with the foster mother in individual and joint therapy during this initial period, soothing tempers and encouraging Carol. Everyone hung in, and Carol, who continued attending counseling regularly, began to learn to channel the energy of her anger into strong assertion skills. She has become a champion for handling conflicts through negotiation and mediation and was instrumental in forming a weekly peer therapy group to be held in the foster home. She is now the oldest kid in her foster home and is looked up to as the voice of experience. She will be graduating from high school in June and also began attending class at a junior college. She plans to major in psychology. A fundamentally intelligent, motivated, socially constructive person is clearly emerging. I sometimes wonder how far she would have gone by now if she had grown up in a supportive home.

Even though Carol has not returned home, her relationship with her mother has improved somewhat. She initially could not speak to her without intense anger and refused to visit her at all. Now she shows good insight into the roots of her anger and even has some compassion for her mother's plight.

I once asked Carol what she would have done if we had not accepted her referral; she answered, "I would be dead. I had the pills ready and had decided to kill myself."

THEN

Viewed historically, public attitudes toward status offenders—runaways, truants, and youth—have changed from a highly restrictive, intrusive viewpoint to acceptance of increasing degrees of behavioral freedom for young people. There has been a reduction in state intervention and more enlightened interpretations of what is deviant or illegal in the deportment of youth. (Status offenses involve conduct by minors that is designated as illegal, although the same actions would not be considered illegal if carried out by adults.) These offenses can be viewed in proscriptive terms (*don't* use alcohol or tobacco), prescriptive terms (*do* obey the commands of your parents), and circumstantial terms (children should not grow up in an environment conducive to "idleness or crime") (Teitelbaum, 1983). Status offenses included such actions of waywardness, curfew violation, using profanity, sexual promiscuity (particularly by girls), and aggressive designation. Status offenders lie in the terrain between children who come to the attention of the court because they have executed a distinct criminal deed and those whose parents have exposed them to abuse or neglect.

There have been three historical waves of runaway phenomena according to Wells and Sandhu (1986), each brought on by broad societal disruption. The first was occasioned by rapid industrialization and urbanization following the colonial period. Another coincided with the Great Depression of the thirties, flowing over into the forties during the period of World War II. The third wave grew out of the counterculture movement of the 1960s and has continued on into the present. This overview of trends will provide context as we go on now to look more specifically at historical aspects of the runaway and homeless issue.

Ancient Origins of Youth Control

The historical roots of current policies for children and youth have been delineated by scholars such as Garlock (1979), Lerman (1980), Rothman (1971), Ryerson (1978), Teitelbaum (1983), and Schlossman (1977). In this discussion only a few salient highlights will be given.

From earliest times parents were given authority—often of a harsh nature—over their offspring. The Roman concept of *potestas* covered the absolute power of the father over his children to the extent of leasing or selling them and putting them into slavery or even to death. The Old Testament propounded filial obedience through the Fifth Commandment, as well as through the Book of Deuteronomy (21:18–21), wherein execution of a son by stoning was permitted if he was judged by community elders to have been "disloyal and defiant" to his parents. This Mosaic law, however, had a relatively liberal cast in that it required sanction by an external group in lieu of total discretion by the father.

The Colonial Period

These restrictive views were carried into the early colonial experience in America. The first law pertaining to unruly children was enacted in the Massachusetts Bay Colony in 1646. Modeled on the Book of Deuteronomy, it allowed the death penalty to be applied to male children over the age of 16 who exhibited stubborn or rebellious behavior. This was an expression of Puritan adherence to social control through the family, and it had, as well, an economic function related to gaining full family participation in farming activities that were essential to life, under extremely adverse conditions.

The Industrialization Period

Large-scale public policy and activity regarding marginal youth did not material-ize until the nineteenth century when burgeoning urbanization, industrialization, immigration, and social and geographic mobility began to make an impact. The traditional mechanisms of primary group social control through the family and small cohesive communities were in disarray. In a social landscape colored by city life and factory culture, norms were less solidified and uniformly accepted. The streets became inundated with disturbing numbers of young children who were idle, without regular homes, prone to criminality, and showing signs of coagulating into "dangerous classes" threatening the viability of the social order. The "elites" of society, nevertheless, gradually came to believe that the children of the poor were salvageable, in need of redirection, and that manipulation of the environment would be the means through which they might be reformed and molded into responsible (and loyal) members of society. With this *weltan-schauung,* deviance could be managed and controlled, even though it might not be rooted out. Such a position was, indeed, more optimistic than the earlier Puritanical posture, which saw wayward children reflecting the fundamental, unalterable sinfulness of humankind.

Houses of Refuge and Reform Schools

This confluence of forces and beliefs gave rise in the early 1800s to the Houses of Refuge, initially in the large eastern coastal cities (New York in 1826, Philadelphia in 1829). Courts could now place ungovernable or vagrant children into specific institutions, where they would receive an appropriate moral education. A regimen of hard work, obedience, and self-discipline would benefit young people and steer them along the proper path. Historian David Rothman (1971: 212) describes the Houses of Refuge as aiming "to enlighten their (inmates') minds, and aid them in forming virtuous habits, that they may finally go forth, clothed as in invincible armor. They would *gird the young to withstand temptation."* The first reform school sprang up in Massachusetts in 1847 and became the major vehicle for youth-oriented correctional work.

Meanwhile, the net widened as the doctrine of *parens patriae* expanded its scope. With the advent of compulsory school attendance laws (beginning in 1853 in New York), truants became candidates for corrective intervention, and the corrupting influences of urban existence led to the inclusion of other very specific acts, such as frequenting gaming houses, brothels, or railroad yards. Children were increasingly being punished for behavior that varied from the norm and were placed in institutional residences together with those who had enacted serious and appalling criminal offenses. While safeguards were beginning to be applied with regard to separating child and adult deviants, no distinctions were being made regarding the extent or character of criminality among different groups of troubled children brought before the courts.

The Juvenile Court

Dissatisfaction with these arrangements built up gradually and culminated in 1899 with the establishment in Chicago of the first juvenile court, an event that was a milestone in organized concern for children. The court was designed to substitute a unified jurisdiction and set of procedures for the existing disorderly means of providing for children. It also aimed for intervention of the state in the lives of children in a caring and beneficent way. This institution would, for the first time, combine the functions of a child welfare service agency and a legal adjudicatory body. Advocates of the court saw an acceleration in a criminal trajectory beginning with exposure to child neglect or, perhaps, engaging in trivial offenses, to carrying out serious criminal transgressions. The juvenile court would scoop up youngsters at an earlier stage and deflect antisocial behavior through rational and humane programs of rehabilitation. Diverse behavioral expressions in youth, therefore, could be signs of a need to receive societal support and guidance, and, since the purpose of intervention was viewed as essentially benign, the scope of the court's reach was painted with very broad strokes. Within these expansive boundaries for defining the domain of the court fell clear acts of a criminal nature, together with such diverse and vaguely conceived areas as disobeying parents or teachers, taking part in "immoral conduct," or "constituting a danger to oneself or others." The altruistic zeal of the court left little room for any potentially needy youngsters to escape from its embrace.

Not only was there a broad definition for receiving the attention of the court, but also forms of disposition were widely drawn. All children could receive all forms of dispensation, since the court's action, after all, was well intentioned, rehabilitative, and highly discretionary. In this way, status offenders and victims of abusing parents could be confined for long periods of time in industrial schools, commingling with youth who perpetrated grave criminal excesses.

These defects in the judicial system should, in no way, blur our understanding of the idealistic purposes of the court and the motives of those who fought for its creation. In truth, it was an offspring of the child reform movement of the late 1800s—a movement that was instrumental in bringing into being child labor laws and universal public education.

The emerging professions of social work, education, and child development played a significant role in shaping the form of the court. Scholars of the psychology of childhood and adolescence, such as G. Stanley Hall and Adolph Mayer, had much to do with its genesis, as did social work pioneers Jane Addams and Julia Lathrop. According to Zatz (1982: 21), the court was conceived according to such principles as:

> Separating juveniles from adult proceedings, establishing individual case dispositions and remedies designed to be therapeutic rather than exclusively punitive, designing specialized police and social service units to deal with

young people, and enacting statutory reforms that further enhanced its jurisdiction. The court set in place a system of considerable magnitude and power. Every young person in need of assistance was eligible for judicial attention.

The Chicago Bar Association, in support, endorsed the right and duty of the state to extend "that tender solicitude and care over its neglected, dependent wards that a wise and loving parent would exercise with reference to his own children under similar circumstances" (Platt, 1970: 139). Judge Mack (1969: 107) of the Chicago court, writing in the *Harvard Law Review,* argued that in dealing with a child it is proper for the court "to find out what he is, physically, mentally, and morally, and then, if it learns that he is treading the path that leads to criminality, to take him in charge, not so much to punish as to reform, not to degrade but to uplift, not to crush but to develop, not to make a criminal but a worthy citizen."

Dissatisfaction with the Juvenile Court

It is often the case that the best of intentions go awry or are superseded over time by new needs or philosophical positions. For half a century the principles and modalities of the juvenile court received broad endorsement. Then, in the 1950s and 1960s, the consensus about the courts rapidly gave way. One line of criticism concerned the treating of status offenders and criminal offenders in a common framework. The labeling of status offenders within a criminal context was decried as detrimental. Children who had committed no real crime would become stigmatized as "bad kids," with multiple harmful effects. Self-perception as a deviant might occur, expanding the individual's definition of what kind of marginal behavior is acceptable.

In addition, since it was not possible to maintain absolute confidentiality about the business of the court and information about young people fell into the hands of numerous external organizations, labeling occurred, often making it difficult for status offenders to gain access to jobs, educational and vocational opportunities, and programs of private social agencies. Beyond that, the commingling in pre- and post-adjudication detention facilities exposed status offenders to a climate of associations and values that could inculcate or support criminal proclivities.

Also, with the rapid deterioration of family life, it was recognized that status offenders were often not norm violators but victims of neglectful, unreasonable, neurotic, or violent parents. Parents, therefore, rather than youth, were acknowledged often to be the prime source of the problematic circumstances of children; add to this a liberalizing philosophy concerning the bounds of appropriate and acceptable behavior on the part of young people. Civil rights and antiwar activities, the counterculture movement, and the drug and rock music phenomena of the 1960s and 1970s all contributed to expanding perspectives on the prerogatives of the young.

Children's Rights and Civil Liberties Factors

A central consideration, at the same time, was the children's rights movement. The United Nations and the National Commission for the Mental Health of Children issued statements on the basic rights of children. The Twenty-Sixth Amendment to the Constitution was ratified in 1971, recognizing eighteen-year-olds as adults. The juvenile court, an institution which had been meant to look after and enhance young people's lives, came to be viewed as a restricting force on the civil rights of children and one that denied them legal protection.

Several significant legal cases began to constrain the prerogatives of the juvenile courts. The Gault ruling—*In re Gault,* 387 U.S. 1 (1967)—pointed up the tension between punishment and rehabilitation that was embodied in the juvenile court from its beginnings. The Gault decision insisted on procedural guarantees for children facing the commitment power of the court. The court was found not to represent the totally benign, rehabilitative force envisioned by its founders but rather to include coercive features against which all citizens, including children, needed legal safeguards. *Kent v. United States,* 383 U.S. 541 (1966), also dealt with due process issues. *Wyatt v. Stickney,* 325 F. Supp. 781 (1971), adjudged institutionalization without proper treatment to be a form of incarceration. Other challenges to the court have included charges of vagueness, overbreadth, and violations of the Eighth Amendment. All of these cases represented a blot to the ubiquitous power exerted by the court and brought into better balance the child welfare and legal components of the court structure.

Toward Deinstitutionalization

In the early 1960s, the doubts and dissatisfactions surrounding the judicial treatment of children resulted in a diverse set of actions. The New York Family Court Act was passed in 1963, establishing a new jurisdictional category for behavior that was not criminal but only illegal for children—Persons in Need of Supervision (PINS). California followed shortly thereafter as the second state to differentiate between criminal and status offenses. This notion diffused rapidly but with nomenclature variations among states—Children in Need of Supervision (CINS), Minors in Need of Supervision (MINS), and Juveniles in Need of Supervision (JINS). While this development divided status and criminal offenders at the preadjudication stage, postadjudication disposition through separate facilities and services was not widely instituted. Commonly, the various types of youth offenders were placed in industrial schools—a special detriment for girls who were disproportionately represented among status offenders. Cost was a consideration here. Preadjudication procedural changes were not financially burdensome; building new, separate facilities for dispositional purposes was.

Meanwhile, political pressure was beginning to be felt by the Kennedy administration in Washington. Delinquency rates were skyrocketing. By 1950 a million and a half youth under eighteen were being arrested annually (Handler and Zatz, 1982). The character of their offenses was becoming more threatening to public safety and tranquility. Crimes of violence (murder, rape, and robbery) were up, as were crimes against property (burglary, larceny, and auto theft). Penal institutions were dangerously overcrowded, and state funds were inadequate for dealing with the crushing demands. John F. Kennedy appointed the President's Commission on Law Enforcement and Administration of Justice in 1967, with a mandate to "enquire into the existing system of juvenile justice." National commissions and standards-setting groups, such as the Joint Commission on Juvenile Justice Standards of the Institute of Judicial Administration, the American Bar Association, and the National Advisory Commission on Criminal Justice and Delinquency Prevention, moved into action. Legislative statutes were enacted, including the Omibus Crime Control and Safe Streets Act of 1968 and the Juvenile Delinquency Prevention and Control Act of 1968.

These currents came together in the Juvenile Justice and Delinquency Prevention Act of 1974, a watershed measure whose impact radically altered legal and community responses to status offenders—an impact that dominates the situation in states and communities across the country to this very day. This act committed the federal government to deinstitutionalization of status offenders and made the federal government a potent force in propagating this philosophy among the states.

Decriminalization of Status Offenders

The Federal Juvenile Justice and Delinquency Prevention Act of 1974 (Pub. L. No. 93–415, 88 Stat. 1109) was multipronged in its approach to deinstitutionalization. Among its most significant features were the following:

1. It limited the placement of status offenders in secure "lock up" facilities for detention and correctional purposes.
2. It disapproved of the commingling of status offenders and criminal offenders in all aspects of the legal and correctional process, as well as the commingling of juveniles and adults at any point.
3. It called for diversion of status offenders from the formal structures of juvenile justice, to the greatest extent possible.
4. It encouraged the use of varied community-based resources for treatment and rehabilitation in place of the mechanisms of the criminal justice system.

The act linked continued federal funding of juvenile offender programs generally (including criminal cases) within the states to compliance with the provisions of the new legislation, allowing for a three-year period of local tooling up. In this way, the act became a powerful lever prodding the states to promulgate decriminalization policies and programs. The new law was consistent with a general societal movement in the direction of decriminalization (as with drug use, gambling, and sex among consenting adults), diversion, and deinstitutionalization (as with mental health, mental retardation, and physical disabilities). Diversion (one of the features of the act) also featured a general tendency to shift the provision of human services to private resources or to promote a greater degree of sharing and cooperation among voluntary and governmental agencies. The role of the courts would be to facilitate and monitor the provision of services to young people who needed them through child welfare agencies, public services, and voluntary social service agencies.

The experience in the fifty states of adopting the philosophy and of mounting the programs related to decriminalization has been uneven and uncoordinated. Sarri states: "The situation is wholly haphazard, with incredible variation within and between the states and with no federal oversight of comprehensiveness or equity" (n.d.: 288).

It has been observed that implementation of decriminalization was adversely affected by the breakup of the coalition that had formed to push the concept through Congress. Several divergent streams of thinking had come together to promote decriminalization. There were, first of all, the civil libertarians and children's rights advocates who wished to restrict the broad-gauged powers of the juvenile courts and to extend legal protections to the young. Then there were the fiscal conservatives who wanted to get the governmentally financed court out of the business of giving costly services to its charges and to shift the burden of expenditure to private sources. Finally, hard-liners on youth care joined in the campaign. For them, withdrawing frills for marginally troubled youth would increase the resources available for tough-minded programs (more industrial schools, longer sentences, and more police on the streets) that would suppress chronically violent and dangerous youth. After the legislative victory on deinstitutionalization, this polyglot group could not find common ground for a concerted effort at implementation. Indeed, their programmatic objectives clashed.

Another observation is that the removal of the court from a position of responsibility for runaway and homeless youth has left a void. No other agency or institution has taken prime or significant responsibility. A result is that the number of runaways aimlessly wandering the streets has skyrocketed. They fall between the cracks of the social service delivery system, free from unfair legal treatment by the criminal justice system but not receiving social treatment and support from the social welfare system.

NOW

One of the few attempts to gather information on the current situation was a study conducted by the U.S. Department of Health and Human Services, Region X, Office of the Inspector General (1983). In this study 345 persons in twelve states were interviewed. The respondents were individuals associated with governmental and voluntary runaway programs, schools, community service agencies, the courts, police, and others.

From these interviews it was estimated that there are 1,155,284 runaway and homeless youth annually in the United States (a conservative figure, the researchers say). Of this number, 73 percent are "locals," 11 percent are from out of the county, and 16 percent are from out of the state. Only one-fifth run away from mildly troubling home environments; the majority break away from deeply disturbing situations—36 percent, from physical or sexual abuse, and 44 percent, from other "severe long-term problems."

Under these adverse conditions, it is estimated that only 50 percent have a realistic prospect of either returning to their own home or to a foster care situation. Fewer than 10 percent are in readiness for emancipation. A particularly disturbing note is the estimate that as many as 25 percent are chronic, hard-core "street kids," rooted in unstable, deviant life-styles, of whom 75 percent engage in criminal activity and 50 percent, in prostitution, specifically. Respondents stated that the current runaway population is more deeply troubled than previously ("more severe," "more screwed up," "tougher," "more multiple problems"). They are also highly vulnerable to exploitation by adults, including areas such as male and female prostitution, pornography, and drug abuse (see Luna, 1987; McMullen, 1986; Price, 1989). Accordingly, they are at high risk for acquiring sexually transmitted diseases, including AIDS (English, 1989; Hersch, 1988; Ritter, 1989).

A number of conclusions were reached concerning the service system for runaways. There was criticism of federal program guidelines that restrict the length of stay in shelters to two weeks; more flexible time lines were considered to be beneficial. There is a dearth of shelters serving ethnic minorities. It was felt that specific programs should focus on targeted segments of the runaway population; mixing runaway types may have detrimental effects. Few programs are equipped to serve seriously disturbed adolescents who are violent, aggressive, or psychotic. A need was indicated for better national systems for gathering and disseminating data, and for providing training and technical assistance to agencies and professionals.

A Youth Development Bureau study (U.S. Department of Health and Human Services, 1980) adds some additional information. Several different categories of runaway and homeless youth are established for analytical purposes: *runaways,* those who leave home without the permission of their parents; *push-outs,* those who leave home with parental encouragement; *throwaways,* those who leave home with parental approval and desire to leave home; and *noncrisis youth,* those living in a problematic situation but not planning to leave. The study found that runaways are the largest category, at 42 percent, followed by push-outs and throwaways (28 percent), and then by noncrisis youth (20 percent). Females outnumber males in each category, except push-outs. The preponderance of youth served are in the fourteen to seventeen age group (83 percent). There is definite representation from the nine- to thirteen-year-olds (13.3 percent). The majority of the clientele are white (72 percent), with blacks comprising 16 percent and Hispanics, 6 percent. The families of these youth, in large proportion, are headed by a single parent or a stepparent (61.7 percent). Referrals to programs are as follows: self, 19 percent, juvenile justice system, 27 percent; and human service agencies, 21 percent.

Several other national scope studies round out the picture of runaway and homeless youth. A congressionally sponsored investigation (Woodside, 1980) determined that a large number of homeless (20 to 35 percent) had been in foster care prior to requesting shelter services. Many of them indicated that sexual abuse had been a cause for leaving home and cited stress caused by parental alcoholism as well. The Opinion Research Corporation (1976) reported that runaway and homeless youth come from both white-collar and blue-collar homes in approximately equal proportions. The same study pointed to substantial police involvement by runaways: 24 percent of them had at least one arrest, compared with 11 percent of a control group. Another study by the Educational Systems Corporation (1978) highlighted the prevalence of parental abuse and neglect among runaways: 58 percent of those surveyed reported being beaten at least once a month; 26 percent, every day. These youth had a diverse set of needs, including shelter, medical care, and advocacy services. Some twenty needed services, in all, were identified. The most pressing of these, noted by 73 percent of the youth, was long-term housing.

This background sketch of the current status of runaway and homeless youth gives a disquieting perspective. These areas will be expanded upon in the chapters that follow. The analysis will also seek out solution strategies and policies.

GETTING ORGANIZED

(Administrators Talk About Their Agencies)

HELPING HANDS AND TEENWORKS:
THE URBAN TO RURAL CONTINUUM

Helping Hands was started back in 1982 and has operated as an arm of Catholic Charities. We're part of a network of agencies in this city that are out in the field working with runaway kids. We didn't start a shelter type of service. What we did was open up field offices about a block and a half away from the bus terminal near the train station, and in the entertainment district. In each of those field offices we have teams that go out and work in the surrounding streets that are in those areas. Kids are coming into a metropolis like this all the time, and we want to get to them before some other people with different motives get to them.

We have two-people teams, a male and female partner who go out together. They walk and they talk, they hand out material, they put up fliers any time that they can get away with it—on anything that's not moving. Their main purpose is to try to identify the young people that are on the streets and zero in on our primary target. That's the "baby" runaway.

We know that the long-term runaways are out there. We do provide services for them. If they are in need of only a sandwich, we'll give them only a sandwich. If they are in need of a change of clothes, we have clothing to offer. If they want to talk, we will talk. If they need some sort of advocacy done, we'll go to bat for them. But our main target is the baby runaway, the young kid that's been on the street maybe a week or two weeks. The way that we spot them is through our teams that are out every day. They are walking the downtown streets. They walk through the parks, they cover shopping malls, abandoned houses, and alleys. These young kids are the most vulnerable and maybe the most amenable to getting back into the family.

21

Once the team makes contact, the approach is very low keyed. It's simply, "Hi, we're from Helping Hands. If you need it, we can provide you with a meal." Or, "Listen, where are you staying tonight?" If the kids look very disheveled, the staff will use whatever they have to use to get into that person's life. Once kids show some sort of interest in our program, they are invited to come to one of the centers. We have clothing. We have food, and we have another counseling team that remains at the center and will work with the kid there.

Our primary object is family reunification. That's the first thing we get around to in talking to the kid. If that's not possible, then we start talking about other programs. We refer the kid to any other program that will be able to provide long-term service.

One of the things we found out about runaways is that they are mobile, they're out there moving around. We're discussing a problem with the state right now. They wanted us to put ramps in and remodel our building to accommodate the handicapped. I told them these kids are able to freely move from one location to the other. They do it without ramps or any other assistance. Most people have heard about the large Covenant House program smack dab in the middle of Times Square. They seem to have thousands of kids outside the door. That's not happening here. Our kids are moving around.

We decided that we had to be mobile, too. So we now have an office on wheels—a mobile crisis center. It's a camper-van that we keep stocked with food and clothing and all the necessary paperwork, also manuals and resource books. And we do the same thing there that other agencies do, except we drive there—to the far reaches of the city where other offices aren't located or can't attract kids.

The same approach is used. The team parks itself someplace and walks, talks, does all the contact-making. When they find kids that need services, they invite them back to their van office and give them food, clothing, and talk to them there. The advantage is that when we make a referral we close the front door, hit the gas pedal, and drive directly to the place so we know the kid got there.

There's a philosophy behind our approach. Just this week I saw graffiti scrolled along the wall where my office is: "You are alone." The word "you" was underlined. And somebody else added to that, "But I'm in control."

So many times when we talk to the kids they give out signals that they're alone. But they feel in control of their lives—at least temporarily —and this is what they want. Many ran to be independent and to have that feeling that Mom and Dad aren't forcing things on them—nor anybody else, for that matter.

We respond to this by being very easy in how we come on —nonthreatening, nonjudgmental. This is what many want. We can point them in the directions that they need to go through our networks.

We see Helping Hands as an intermediate step in the process of taking kids off the streets and steering them back home or putting them into a program or a shelter. We're not a treatment center, and we don't intend to be a treatment center. At this point, we just want to be that intermediate step. We say, "You have to go from point 'A' to point 'B' and we can help you get there." We don't want to maintain ownership of our client. We want to pass them on to somebody else, whether it's a team canteen, medical clinic, or job training program. Getting them back to the family would be best most of the time. You can say we're a front-line mobile unit type of operation, like the medics who pick up the injured and take them to where they can get necessary healing.

*   *   *   *

When we started Teenworks some people were surprised. Hancock is your basic small town. No more than 25,000 people live here. And it's rural, in an agricultural county with nothing much else going on. You may think it's an unlikely place for runaway issues and other big-city problems. Well, I know about those urban problems, and I can tell you we have our share. I can also tell you that involving the kids in solving the problems is one of the best ways I know of to make a dent.

Back when I was a kid, it wasn't "in" to be called a hoodlum. But I was, and all my friends were out of control—away from home a lot. Western College decided to come down into the "inner city" with a whole team of folks, and they said, "You, my friend (they were talking to me) are culturally dis—something." I was poor, I was Mexican, so they thought I was sure to strike out. And I said, "What does this mean?" They said, "Well, what we have for you, friend, is a *program!*"

You know, today I was at a United Way meeting all day, and I came back overloaded. Have you ever been to a United Way meeting? There were Eagle Scouts everywhere in that room! I couldn't relate to anybody. I thought, will somebody please swear or cough or have scuffy shoes? But you want to know about our runaway program. I'm working my way up to that.

In Hancock we have a lot of heroin, PCP, crack, marijuana, weed, grass, and other stuff. It's amazing. You go into this place thinking: "I'm going to move here, because this is where my grandfather grew up." My Mom would have loved to have a tree in the yard that grew fruit. We lived on a street that had one tree! But in Hancock we have cherry trees, apricots, and all the kids hang out at the parks. Yet those kids are runaways, and they remind me of *me* in 1959. They're out there on the streets, hustling, doing anything they can to live.

In Hancock we are in a real transitional stage. We're becoming a bedroom community. What you are seeing in the cities, we're starting to see in the country! We live 30 miles south of an industrial county, and we're running into some street kids now that are having real problems.

You may think there aren't that many unjointed kids out there. Well, you'd be surprised. These kids live out in orchards, they live up in the hills, they live in old abandoned cars. In 1959, if someone had said, "Manuel, in a few years from now you're going to be the director of an agency that serves a lot of people, you're going to wear a coat and tie and go to United Way meetings," I would have said, "Bullshit."

But now I have to think about programs, like these Western College people did. For me it's different. I see things through a different lens. When I hear about programs to fight crime, I turn the target in the opposite direction. Crime in the streets! That's what we grew up with. Chicanos and blacks and Indians and the folks who have come over from Asia, they know about crime in the streets. They're exploited, all the time, every day. It's the crime against them that they live with and have to struggle against.

What I learned from the Western College encounter is that you don't just move in and dump a program on people. You have to let them bring in their own view of the world. Let me illustrate. We've had a dramatic increase in suicidal kids. We had about twenty-six attempts last year; the year before, we had twelve. We're talking about kids ages eleven to seventeen who are taking serious steps to terminate their lives. Incidentally, two were successful; we had two suicides in our small county.

What we're doing at Teenworks is developing a youth task force. We've got a bunch of kids together, not the church choir or the debating team at school. Half of this group isn't even attending school on a regular basis. The other half is in alternative education programs because they can't make it in the regular school programs. These kids are from all different backgrounds—runaways, street kids, drug pushers. Some live in group homes or foster homes. We got them together because a little gal who was suicidal and decided that she wanted to turn her life around spoke to others and decided together to harness their energy. These kids have drive and ability, and they have a right to make some decisions in their community. They have a right to be heard, to tell us what they need, so we can develop programs, policies, and activities to meet those needs.

These kids together are doing some incredible things. They are doing outreach for youth. When Teenworks requested funds from the city councils in the county for our programs, these kids attended council meetings. They've met with mayors, some council folks, the chief of police, both in meetings and afterwards standing around informally out in the hall. And they're getting known and putting their ideas across. They are getting some power. They're turning their experiences and troubles into a way to make the community a better place to live.

The other day I got a frantic call from the regional runaway council asking for letters to the governor to support a Runaway and Homeless Act that's coming up. I said, "I'm going to do one better: I'm going to have the kids write letters! The kids receiving the services, the kids that have been on the run, the kids that know." These kids sat down and wrote letters that would blow your mind. I saved copies of all of them; they are beautiful. They wrote letters to the governor about what it's like to be on drugs, not to have a place to live, to be on the street, to have difficulty at home, to be abused, to have tried to take your life.

We're taking this a step further. We are going to be doing leadership training with the group. They want to go out to the schools to talk to other kids about services, tell where they can get help, let them know that they don't have to be adrift on the streets.

I'm taken with these kids. I, for one, would like to see broad youth participation in all community agencies. It's important to let kids have a sense of their own destiny, to have them come to understand they can help themselves and one another. After all, it's their lives. They don't need a program laid on them by some benefactors from the outside.

Characteristics of Runaway and Homeless Youth

CASE IN POINT

(Practitioners Talk About Their Work with Clients)

WILMA

I first met Wilma two years ago at our county teen service center when she was fifteen. A beautiful girl, heavily made up, she appeared much older. I found out why when she told about her past in a monotone, as if she were speaking about someone unrelated to herself.

Sexual abuse and parental neglect were a mark of her early childhood years, together with substance abuse later on. As a black youngster growing up in a racially mixed community on the fringe of the inner city, opportunities for those vices were all around her. Starting at age nine, she'd ended up on the streets, prostituting. It is no wonder that she escalated to an alcohol habit that her psychiatrist described to me as "the worst case I've ever seen in a child her age." She had just completed a two-month stay at a drug program in a hospital psychiatric unit, was "clean and sober," and was staying at a runaway shelter when she blurted out to me, "I want to get my life together."

I placed Wilma in a county residential drug program, where she stayed for about three weeks. Wilma somehow had keen instincts for what she needed, and this wasn't it. So she left, calling me that day to let me know where she was. I placed her in another drug program, where she stayed for several months. Again she left, saying it put too much emphasis on monitoring what she did and not enough on how she *felt*. She decided she wanted to return to a residential alcohol program where she'd gone as an outpatient before, where she knew the people and the program and felt comfortable. Since this wasn't a county-licensed facility, her mother made the agreement with them, and I closed the case. Wilma would call me periodically to let me know how she was doing. I hoped this situation would quell her penchant to be always in motion.

About nine months later, she called to say she and her mother had progressed in family counseling to the point where everyone felt it was time for her to return home. But in a few weeks both Wilma and her mother called. The lack of bonding between them and the years of estrangement had taken their toll. Wilma had skipped out to the home of a friend. She asked if she could stay there officially with me as her social worker again. I visited the home and certified it as licensable, and Wilma's mother signed a voluntary placement agreement. Wilma had gone through the alcohol program with her friend, and they were buddies. It seemed like a nice family, who really wanted to help Wilma.

All went well until the friend moved out into her own apartment after a heated altercation with her father. Wilma was left alone, the only "daughter" in a family with its own set of issues too powerful for Wilma to be a part of. She left again, calling me from a temporary shelter to which she ran. In the past week, we have been dissecting the situation together from every possible psychological angle. Wilma has developed a special sense of perception about what goes on between people and is beginning to be connected to her own feelings through our talks. She is also beginning to understand what her running signifies. Throughout these past two years, her recurring theme song has been, "I don't want to go back to the streets." She says this to herself almost as a mantra. I sense that each place she runs from has not offered her the "perfection" she's searching for. She's keen to every nuance of behavior, and her body and soul seem to seek the peace they've never had; therefore, she continues a stance of rejection because nothing in reality can offer what lives in her fantasy. I've noticed this with many of the other kids who run. They seem to be seeking the ultimate in parenting, but, because they've been so deprived, nothing can fill the emptiness—they keep running: "If I can't get the best, I'll take nothing."

Wilma is beginning to realize this intellectually. She is preparing herself to stay at the next placement until she's eighteen, so that she can achieve her goal of being independent. She has agreed before to not run until she talks to me about what's going on, and perhaps this time she will be able to make it. We've been discussing how well she's been doing, considering the emotional handicaps she's operated with. Throughout it all, she has continued to go to school, has not relapsed into drug and alcohol use, has attended AA groups religiously, and most important, has not returned to the streets. She has not yet completed the ninth grade because of all the missed years of school, but she is set on finishing. Even though she and her mother can't live together, they are developing a reasonable relationship and see each other regularly. Her mother appears to be as emotionally deprived as her daughter and therefore probably was never able to give her child what she needed.

For these reasons, even though Wilma is again in a shelter, awaiting still yet another in her sequence of placements, to me she is a symbol of courage and determination. I believe the steady hand I was able to offer has made a difference to her. As I think about what I've represented to Wilma, a lot of it boils down to being a thread of adult dependability and understanding out in the world. She has experienced me as someone she felt she could really talk to but also someone who is a part of the system and has the desire and the power to do something for her. By not feeling so alone and neglected, she seems to have gathered the wherewithal to work her way beyond the desperate early years, with no real family base to stand on, and to build off of the special vitality she has as a human being. I won't belittle what I've done for Wilma and the degree to which I have extended myself for her. But considering the low point she had to start from, what I have given toward Wilma's achievements pales beside the remarkable contributions she herself has made.

Research on the characteristics of runaway–homeless youth and on truants comes from various sources, uses a variety of different empirical investigation methods, and is broad in the scope of the subject matter that is covered. The findings are organized into five major generalizations, each of which has various subgeneralizations or component parts. The discussion centers on the following topical areas: Typologies of Runaways, Reasons for Running, Self-Concepts of Runaways, Family Factors Among Runaways, and Correlates of Truancy.

This chapter establishes a format, which is also used in Chapter 3. A generalization in italic type is suggested. Following each generalization is a description of some of the studies and contexts from which the generalization was drawn. This, in turn, is followed by a "derived" action guideline. For the reader who wishes to consider the essence of the analysis, without going into the details of the individual studies, the best plan would be to concentrate on the italicized generalizations and the action guidelines that follow.

Because much of the existing research is tenuous and the procedures adopted here, like all social research, have their limitations, the findings and action guidelines ought to be considered tentative and suggestive. They essentially provide serious *ideas* to be taken into consideration in policy and program design, by informed individuals, who can bring judgment and familiarity with the local situation to bear in determining if and how to apply the ideas.

Not only does judgment need to be exerted in the application process, but also follow-up monitoring and evaluation are necessary in order to assess how these intervention approaches impact the local setting and to implement the components of the program. This encourages careful testing and quality control of the programs before they are widely used in practice, and it allows successful program techniques to be delineated and packaged before they are widely disseminated.

In many instances, this synthesis of research leads to conclusions and policies that will seem familiar to observers and professionals in the field and may in this sense be judged to be obvious or just plain "common sense." This is a natural, defensible reaction. However, over the years ideas and practices in the human services field that were considered to be truisms have been discounted when exposed to empirical research scrutiny or to new insights by professionals. Professional fads and "in" practices sometimes substitute for validated interventions. The selection of clients by agencies, for example, has penalized those most in need of service. Long-term therapy was sometimes applied to problems that respond best to short-term structured treatment. Adoption practices were found to be too rigid. The commitment to drawing up long-term, comprehensive plans was found to inhibit effective community planning. The list could be expanded manyfold.

Generalization I: There is no agreed upon typology for runaways. Typologies reflect differing definitions and concepts of runaway behavior. Runaway behavior seems to constitute a multiplex phenomenon. Some of the suggested criteria include:

1. The intended *length of stay* away from home (English, 1973; Jones, 1988; Kufeldt and Nimmo, 1987).
2. The *personal and social characteristics* that include behavioral and attitudinal factors of runaways and/or their parents, success in school, and peer networks (Dunford and Brennan, 1976; Jones, 1988; Crystal, 1986; Ferran and Sabatini, 1985).
3. *Cognitive structure and belief system* (Denoff, 1987; Hartman, Burgess, and McCormack, 1987; Brothers, 1986).
4. Whether running is *self-initiated or youth are push-outs or castaways* (Gullotta, 1978; Pietropinto, 1985).
5. Whether there is an *escalation to criminal offenses* (Boisvert and Wells, 1980).

The concept "runaway" has been challenged as too simple to describe adequately this group of status offenders; numerous typologies have been suggested by Dunford and Brennan, English, and Gullotta. These classifications call into question the intuitive, single-dimension concepts this term provokes. However, there is no consistency among the bases of these typologies, each of which stresses a different aspect of runaway behavior, thereby confirming the inherent complexity.

English presents a typology based on the determined length of time spent away from home. The largest group in adolescent street culture are the "floaters," those who spend relatively short periods of time on the streets and who do not have specific reasons for leaving home, thus going into and out of the runaway population. The next group on an escalating scale of intentionality are those runaways who have left for a specific reason. Many of these adolescents are getting out of a destructive family environment, some are running for altruistic reasons, and there are those who English claims have a "secret" reason. The third group are the "splitters," those who intend to leave home permanently, thereby increasing the number of runaways. The last group, the "hard-road freaks," are making the streets their life. They are the most streetwise of all these groups and are, according to English, mostly from working-class backgrounds.

Dunford and Brennan particularly stress that runaway behavior is not unitary but rather is multidimensional. Their typology combines both behavioral and attitudinal factors, and they suggest six different runaway profiles: self-confident and unrestrained runaway youth; well-adjusted runaway youth; youth who have failed at home and in school, and who are involved in delinquent behavior; youth who are fleeing excessive parental control; young, highly regulated and negatively influenced youth; young and unrestrained youth. Only those who have failed at home and in school, and who are involved in delinquent behavior, and those who are fleeing parental control, had characteristics commonly associated with runaway behavior. The self-confident and unrestrained girls, and the young and unrestrained youth, had an unusually large amount of freedom at home compared with other runaway types. It must be presumed that problems and motivations for running away among these groups are quite different.

These typologies do not address other problems associated with the blanket designation "runaway." In one study, only 30 percent of 368 randomly chosen subjects in a runaway housing program met the National Center for Health definition of runaways, that is, adolescents leaving home or staying away on purpose, knowing they would be missed, and intending to stay away from home for some time. Many of those designated as runaways were more appropriately termed "castaways" because they had been forced from their homes. Some adolescents use runaway housing facilities because other agencies do not offer services these youth need or want (Gullotta, 1978).

Runaways are classified as status offenders, and there is some concern about the escalation of behavior that transforms a status offender into a juvenile delinquent. However, escalation cannot be assumed as an outcome, because sometimes it does not occur. Status offenders are those beginning and finishing as runaways, truants, or stubborn children; some do begin as status offenders and progress to criminal behavior; others move in the opposite direction. The latter begin with delinquent behavior and are later classified as status offenders (Boisvert and Wells, 1980).

Action Guideline 1: There is a need to define more precisely the population constituting runaways, including the various subdivisions of the population. No one program seems adequate to service this complex adolescent population. There need to be many components to a service program, each of which addresses the problems of specific and different populations. Given limited resources, alternatively, specific subpopulations can be selected for targeted, intensive attention.

Diagnosis and differential service programs might take into account, among other things, the intended or actual length of stay away from home, behavioral and attitudinal attributes of runaways and their parents, the degree of school success or adjustment, their peer networks, whether the separation from home is self-initiated or parent imposed, and if engaging in criminal behavior may reasonably be predicted.

Generalization II: The reasons for running away are multiple and complex, including:

1. *Negative psychological or social adjustment* (Reilly, 1978; Kratcoski, 1974; Kammer and Schmidt, 1987; Ferran and Sabatini, 1985). This may vary for males and females (Bartollas, 1975; Kessler and Wieland, 1970; Kratcoski, 1974; Reilly, 1978).
2. *A rational and appropriate reaction to detrimental circumstances* (Aptekar, 1989).
3. *An attempt to find a value system that the runaway can accept* (Adams and Munro, 1979; Loeb, Burke, and Boglarsky, 1986; Reilly, 1978; Williams, 1982). This may include meaning, adventure, and compatible friends.
4. *An attempt to "find" oneself or gain control over one's life* (Adams and Munro, 1979; Brennan, Huizinga, and Elliot, 1978).
5. *Family disturbance—poor communication and parent-child conflict* (Adams and Munro, 1979; Blood and D'Angelo, 1974; Gullotta, 1978; Kammer and Schmidt, 1987; Kogan, 1980; Morgan, 1982; Ferran and Sabatini, 1985).
6. *Parental rejection or expulsion* (Pietropinto, 1985; Gullotta, 1978; Levine, Metzendorf, and VanBoskirk, 1986; Adams, Gullotta, and Clancy, 1985).
7. *Economic stress; lack of adequate resources to sustain a stable pattern of life* (Aptekar, 1989; Ferran and Sabatini, 1985).

The traditional view of runaways as pathological deviants, lacking both stability and the courage to face difficult situations, appears to be confirmed by some researchers, while it is challenged by others. Reilly (1978) reports that runaway girls are more aggressive, angry, impulsive, unstable, easily annoyed, and depressed (some to the point of being preoccupied with suicide) than nonrunaways of the same age. Also, they usually lie and steal more (most often from their mothers) and are truants. It has also been suggested that runaway girls have a history of severe deprivation and neglect compared with boys (Kratcoski, 1974). Reilly (1978) reports that the runaway girls he talked to assumed that leaving home would allow them a more autonomous social life, and they ran to an environment where experimentation with sexual activity and drugs was tolerated.

But other researchers claim that girls run away because of a desire to find security, not adventure (Kessler and Wieland, 1970). It is suggested that boys, however, may have different reasons. One study reports that they may become runaways when faced with unmanageable problems that they feel they cannot handle (Bartollas, 1975).

Adams and Munro (1979) argue that the model of all runaways as pathological deviants is very difficult to prove from the research findings. They suggest two other categories. An alternative values model suggests that adolescents react to the social standards imposed by their family, school, and so on by running away to another life. Thus, they leave home to find both meaning and adventure. In the deindividuation model, teenagers run away in order to find themselves. Adolescents embroiled in parental conflict need to separate themselves from the family situation in order to develop their own individual identity.

However, parent-child conflict is only one aspect of the problem. Williams (1982) points out the importance of peers. She argues that running away is best understood in terms of a value similarity model. Runaways have friends who share their views of the world; they run to a place where their values and behavior are accepted. This corroborates Reilly's statement, referred to earlier, that runaway girls seek an environment where their values are accepted.

It is generally agreed that conflict with parents is a primary reason for leaving home (Adams and Munro, 1979; Blood and D'Angelo, 1974; Gullotta, 1978; Kogan, 1980; Morgan, 1982). Although all teenagers perceive conflicts as dichotomized into major or minor issues, status offenders identified more issues as major and reported more conflict with their parents than nonstatus offenders (Blood and D'Angelo, 1974). One study in which a thirty-nine-item scale was used showed that runaways report more conflict with their parents than nonrunaways on thirty-eight of the items. The only area in which there was less conflict concerned going to college (Blood and D'Angelo, 1974). Disturbances with parents typically center around parental control and concern over such issues as disapproval of boyfriend or girlfriend, grooming, dress, school, and behavior (Gullotta, 1978).

Finally, some of the explanations suggested above are combined and given a different perspective by Brennan, Huizinga, and Elliot (1978). They propose two models to account for runaway behavior. One model, the "strain" perspective, suggests that running away is a response to real or anticipated problems at home that the youth perceives are a result of his or her personal failure. Such adolescents have emotional bonds with, and commitment to, their families, but the relationship is threatened by some crisis or stressful situation. For these adolescents, fleeing can be viewed as an attempt to draw attention to the home situation with the hope that it will precipitate some resolution of the problems. These youths usually stay away for a short time only and then voluntarily return home.

The second model, the "control" perspective, describes behavior that also originates with the family, but here the youth do not have strong bonds with, or commitment to, their families. There can be many reasons for this, but the general point is that early social mechanisms were absent or weak. These youth feel minimal attachment to the family and are attracted to external groups and environments. They transfer their loyalties to a peer group on whom they depend for the satisfaction of their personal and social needs. Usually involved in multiple and long-term episodes of running away, such adolescents do not want to return home, often exhibit delinquent behavior, and have frequent contact with police.

Action Guideline II: The findings that identify multiple reasons for running away again suggest that support services must be varied and flexible. Psychological counseling appears to be a strong program requirement, although it might take different forms for boys and girls. Girls appear to be more acting out and emotionally distraught, suggesting more extensive therapy. Some runaways need help particularly in clarifying their value systems and in gaining self-insight for personal identification. The differences in the problems and needs of runaways, depending upon whether they flee to draw attention to problems at home as a way of alleviating them or to find ways of living independently of the family, must be taken into account.

Even when youth can return home, family counseling appears to be necessary. Programs are needed both to facilitate family reunion and to aid youth in achieving emancipation from the family.

If runaways do flee to peers because they share their values, it would be useful if services, or access to services, were available where teenagers congregate, that is, through teen organizations, clubs, and places where they "hang out." These findings highlight the use of peer culture as a program tool, either in terms of group homes for self-directed living or utilization of peer counselors.

Before leaving this section, in which values were described as important, it would be useful to acknowledge that adolescents, in general, have a value system different from that of the rest of society, including music, dress, language, and so on. Even within this adolescent subculture, a number of different subpopulation value systems can be identified (Blood and D'Angelo, 1974; Heck, 1980; Williams, 1982). Adolescence is a difficult stage to go through, and diverse problems must be faced. Rather than focusing only on adolescents' low self-confidence and poor self-images, Heck (1980) argues that the teen stage in life must be considered. He states that status offenses are best viewed in terms of teenagers trying to cope with their adolescent status in society.

It would be advantageous for everyone working with status offenders to be well trained in adolescent psychology and cognizant of the most recent research and theory concerning teenage attitudes, confusions, and strivings. It seems desirable that everyone who is concerned with providing services to adolescents be in direct contact with them on at least an occasional basis, if not in a regular fashion.

Generalization III: Runaways have poorer self-images and less self-confidence than nonrunaways (Adams and Munro, 1979; Englander, 1984; Levinson and Mezei, 1970; McMullen, 1986; Miller, 1981; Reilly, 1978; Shinohara and Jenkins, 1967; Wolk and Brandon, 1977).

Status offenders usually have poorer self-concepts and interpersonal relations, have more self-doubt, and are more anxious and defensive than nonrunaways (Levinson and Mezei, 1970; Miller, 1981; Shinohara and Jenkins, 1967; Wolk and Brandon, 1977). They also have less social poise and feel as though they lack control of their environment when they are compared with nonrunaways (Adams and Munro, 1979; Englander, 1984). As stated earlier, in a comparison with nonrunaway girls, runaway girls were found to be more unstable and suicidal.

Action Guideline III: Runaways may need sustained counseling regarding self-image, self-confidence, and interpersonal relationships. Services to girls may need to be more intensive and broadly applied. Whether such services would alter runaway tendencies is uncertain, but as a group this population appears to be in considerable need of ego and environmental support.

Generalization IV: Families of runaways are frequently dysfunctional in one way or another. The following difficulties have been identified:

1. *Parents are separated, divorced, in trouble with the law, or abusing alcohol* (Byles, 1980; Datesman and Scarpitti, 1975; Grinnel and Loftis, 1977; Kratcoski, 1974; Kohn and Sugarman, 1978; Zabczynska, 1977).
2. *The structure of the family may be problematic.* For example, if the family is larger than average or if there are many younger siblings, this can exacerbate adolescent problems (Johnson and Peck, 1978).
3. *Runaways perceive themselves as unloved or unwanted by their families* (Adams and Munro, 1979; Blood and D'Angelo, 1974; Englander, 1984; Jenkins, 1971; Johnson and Peck, 1978; Reilly, 1978; Spillane-Grieco, 1984; Tsubouchi and Jenkins, 1969; Wolk and Brandon, 1977).

4. *Sexual and physical abuse can be occurring or may have occurred* (Daly and Wilson, 1985; Gullotta, 1978; Janus, Burgess, and McCormack, 1987; McCormack, Burgess and Hartman, 1988; James, 1977; Reilly, 1978).
5. *The adolescent may become a scapegoat and divert attention away from other problems in the family* (Curry, Autry, and Harris, 1980; Druckman, 1979; Datesman and Scarpitti, 1975; Kogan, 1980).

Family dysfunction may affect boys and girls differentially. However, findings are unclear on this (Adams and Munro, 1979; Englander, 1984).

Many studies are concerned with the problems parents have and how these affect adolescents. The Moos Family Environmental Scale was administered to status offender families in St. Louis, Missouri (Kogan, 1980). It was shown that these families had above average scores for conflict, low cohesion scores, and below average scores on all personal growth dimensions. Studies show that the most prevalent family conditions of runaways include separated parents, parents in conflict with the law, alcohol abuse by one or both parents, and/or physical violence by one or both parents (Byles, 1980; Datesman and Scarpitti, 1975; Zabczynska, 1977). A disrupted home situation was identified in 59 percent of the girls and 45 percent of the boys in one study (Kratcoski, 1974), and 50 percent of the parents were divorced or legally separated in another (Grinnell and Loftis, 1977). An exception to this was found among Hawaiian or part-Hawaiian adolescents with only one parent, who were found to be less likely to become chronic runaways than other adolescents in Hawaii (Mathews and Ilon, 1980).

One study comparing the differences in characteristics among runaways, truants, and delinquent offenders suggests that the Persons in Need of Supervision (PINS) status offenders were involved in more serious family crises and more likely to suffer overt parental rejection. These families, too, seemed more confused over role expectations (Kohn and Sugarman, 1978).

A poor relationship with parents does not seem to be affected by birth position in the family but does somewhat correlate with family size. Runaways are often from larger families and many have very young siblings. In one study, 19 percent had siblings under five years of age and 45 percent had siblings under seven years of age (Johnson and Peck, 1978). Researchers suggest that this family configuration results in decreased parental attention for the older children and increased sibling rivalry for attention. More than 25 percent of the runaways in one study were from families in which all the other siblings were of the opposite sex. It was assumed that in such cases the "different" child feels isolated and alienated from other family members and is more likely to become a runaway (Johnson and Peck, 1978).

While parents report that runaways will not obey them, cooperate with them, or come home on time (Kogan, 1980), the children report more parental rejection than for nonrunaways. They say their parents neither listen to them nor care about them, that they are not supportive or empathetic, and are too strict (Adams and Munro, 1979; Blood and D'Angelo, 1974; Englander, 1984; Jenkins, 1971; Johnson and Peck, 1978; Reilly, 1978; Spillane-Grieco, 1984; Tsubouchi and Jenkins, 1969; Wolk and Brandon, 1977).

Results of studies on the relationship between girls running away from home and the occurrence of incest in that home are very mixed. In one small study, all the girls said the experience of incest was partially responsible for their "subsequent delinquency." The males who were involved were all fathers or stepfathers (James, 1977). In a larger study, an association between running away and overtly incestuous incidents between the girl and her father or father substitute was found (Reilly, 1978). In the largest study, only four cases of parent-child sexual relations were identified out of a total sample of 348 (Gullotta, 1978). However, it should be pointed out that these studies were methodologically different. The small study involved intensively personal case studies by a psychotherapist, with whom girls might feel free to reveal intimate information, whereas the largest study involved the analysis of formal records of a runaway shelter program.

However, differences in family situations occur not only between runaways and nonrunaways but also, perhaps, between runaway boys and runaway girls. The data comparing boys and girls are variable. Generally, girls report they are subject to more parental control and stricter punishment than boys. As a consequence, many girls claim to experience more conflict and stress than do boys (Adams and Munro, 1979), but various studies have generated different results. In Wolk and Brandon's (1977) comparison with nonrunaways, runaway girls report the highest, and runaway boys the lowest, degree of parental control. But, in another study, runaway girls reported their parents were less restrictive and less supportive than the parents of nonrunaways (Englander, 1984), and parents of runaway girls have also been described as punitive and permissive (Reilly, 1978).

Finally, it has been suggested that families of juvenile status offenders lack some degree of family orientation. Families of female status offenders have been described as only somewhat cohesive and adaptive (Druckman, 1979), and lacking in emotional closeness among the members (Kogan, 1980). A method of measuring family dysfunction is Minuchin's structural model of the family, which delineates three subsystems—spouse, parental, and sibling. Using the model, one study of status offenders found that the spouse subsystem was dysfunctional in each case (Curry, Autry, and Harris, 1980). The problems within the spouse subsystem weakened the parental subsystem. Thus, attending to the difficulties of the status offender served to provide a diversion from the troubled marital relationship and to hold the marriage together (Curry, Autry, and Harris, 1980; Kogan, 1980). The sibling subsystem also proved generally to be dysfunctional. The young status offender often strongly identifies with older siblings who reinforce the status offense behavior (Curry, Autry, and Harris, 1980).

Action Guideline IV: Since many runaways come from disorganized and precarious families, obviously it is often not sufficient to deal with the status offender alone. The family may need to be involved in the search for a solution to the various problems. Assisting the family may require dealing with parental conflict, divorce, alcoholism, legal problems, sexual abuse, or the scapegoating and/or abusing of a particular child. Youth problems to be dealt with may include being one of many children, having no other siblings of the same sex, living with an unsympathetic stepparent, or feeling unloved and unwanted in the family. For a child to return to the family, appropriate family support seems to be essential in many cases.

Another programmatic implication is that parenting skills should be taught in problematic situations as well as to the general population, in order to avoid some of the family difficulties identified in the findings. When family dysfunction is evident, an assessment of the subsystems (spouse, parental, sibling) would be diagnostically useful (Curry, Autry, and Harris, 1980; Druckman, 1979).

Truant behavior has been identified as a precursor of runaway behavior. Young people with family problems or psychological stress often play out their difficulties initially in their school setting, frequently by way of absence from school. Truancy, then, is both an early warning symptom and, if unresolved, a cause of running away.

Generalization V: Truants have been found to have particular characteristics related to school, peers, parents, and teachers, including:

1. *Engaging in confrontations in school* (Zieman and Benson, 1980).
2. *Difficulties with authorities* (Nielsen and Gerber, 1979; Zieman and Benson, 1980).
3. *Educational problems—a lack of academic success* (Berg et al., 1978; Miller, 1981; Zieman and Benson, 1980; Levine, Metzendorf, and VanBoskirk, 1986).
4. *A lack of sociocultural relevance for minority group truants* (Haro, 1977).
5. *Social isolation in the school—"peer phobic"* (Berg et al., 1978; Miller, 1981; Nielsen and Gerber, 1979; Levine, Metzendorf, and VanBosirk, 1986).
6. *Overprotective parents who have complicity with truant behavior* (Berg et al., 1978; Little and Thompson, 1983).
7. *Rejecting parents* (Little and Thompson, 1983).

The behavioral problems of junior high school truants have been shown to be related to their perception of school as associated with confrontations and authority strains (Nielsen and Gerber, 1979; Zieman and Benson, 1980). Acts of truancy are viewed as "authority defying" (Nielsen and Gerber, 1979).

Educational difficulties appear in truant profiles (Berg et al., 1978). The lack of academic success plays a part in the truancy of junior high school students (Zieman and Benson, 1980), and truants often need to repeat a grade (Miller, 1981).

An ethnographic study of truant Chicano students with low academic success found that truants found little in the sociocultural characteristics of the institution that related to the Chicano (Haro, 1977). Truant participants in the study reacted negatively toward the formal subsystem that included the teachers, the curriculum, and the school's organizational structure (Haro, 1977).

Truants also express a "peer phobic" reaction by not attending school (Nielsen and Gerber, 1979). In studies of truant characteristics, social isolation was manifested in having few friends (Berg et al., 1978), with the truant student also perceiving negative labeling by peers (Miller, 1981).

Parents of truants have been found to be overprotective and overindulgent (Little and Thompson, 1983). Parental contributions to truancy may also take the form of encouraging nonattendance and subsequent complicity with acts of truancy (Berg et al., 1978).

Little and Thompson also evaluated the attitudes and behaviors of teachers. They found that teachers of junior high school truants may reject and overprotect truant students (Little and Thompson, 1983).

Action Guideline V: Since truancy has multiple causes and truants are not a homogeneous group, a variety of different approaches is necessary to assist them with their problems. They may need counseling to deal with their confrontational behavior and difficulties with authority figures. This could include techniques to build self-discipline and appropriate cooperative behavior. Alternatively, mediation among relevant parties may be a useful technique.

In some situations, advocacy may be necessary to correct adverse school conditions, either by teaching truants effective advocacy skills or by advocating on their behalf. This may be especially true for minority students.

Other students may need assistance in forming better interpersonal and social relationships. Helping students to become part of informal networks or to join established formal groupings and clubs could be of value.

Providing emotional support or academic tutoring may be the appropriate treatment choice for some students.

In some cases, the focus of attention should be parents or teachers. Parents who have overprotected or abetted truant behavior should be assisted to gain a better perspective of their role and its consequences. Teachers should be helped to understand how their overprotective or disdainful reactions may contribute to truancy and to modify their interaction with these students accordingly.

Resolving truancy problems at an early point will, for some youngsters, be decisive in heading off escalation to the level of runaway behavior or criminal delinquency.

GETTING ORGANIZED

(Administrators Talk About Their Agencies)

LAMBERT HOUSE

Lambert House is a professional, interdisciplinary, multiservice program for teenage girls with severe emotional and behavioral problems. And there are more of these youngsters around and needing help than most people have any idea about. At any given time in our city, about 7,000 adolescents ages eleven to eighteen are living in an out-of-home situation, a group home, foster family, Juvenile Hall, or an intensive treatment program. They are victims of unstable or broken families, of abuse, of neglect and abandonment. Many of them have suffered physical or sexual abuse.

They are the kids you see hanging out at fast-food restaurants and who are arrested for shoplifting, vandalism, and other crimes. They are the ones who fail in school because they can't concentrate or remain quiet for a full class period. They feel worthless, they drink and do drugs, and they harm themselves in other self-destructive ways. Their symptoms can range from low self-esteem, to behavior problems, to suicide.

The Lambert House residential treatment program assists those adolescents who have been among the most severely damaged by their experiences. The program focuses on the fourteen to seventeen age group. These adolescents have a basic need for understanding and affection, for counseling and therapy, and for a stable environment where they can begin to regain control over their lives. In many ways, the young people at Lambert House are at a crossroads. Many are bright and full of life, but, without care and assistance, they face a very uncertain future.

Youth are referred to the program by the Children's Bureau, the Department of Probation, and other sources. They are screened by the intake worker to determine the suitability of the program for them. The average length of stay in the program is seven months. Most girls leave following their graduation from high school or on turning eighteen. Many of the girls reunite with their families; other achieve an independent life-style.

The residential treatment program is staffed by forty-five employees providing 24-hour care, professional care, and administrative and support services. A team of volunteers enriches the program in a variety of ways. The building housing the program was originally a magnificent private home. There are thirty girls' rooms, including three triple rooms for new residents, for a total of thirty-six spaces. The wings are divided into three "units," offering a smaller social environment, designed to provide a personal home atmosphere for the girls.

Resident counselors are on hand for 24-hour care. They work with a particular unit and develop close relationships with these girls. Five counselors are on duty in the evenings, and three at night and during the day (when most of the girls are in school). The resident counselors talk and socialize with the girls, check that house rules are followed, solve particular problems, and help make sure that each girl is doing okay at all times.

The program is operated on a "level" system: the girls earn privileges, such as a larger allowance or permission to go to the movies, according to their behavior. There are six levels, and each week, at a regular meeting, each girl's behavior is reviewed. If she has done well, she can graduate to the next level of privilege. The level system makes for a structured environment for each of the girls. It encourages those who are ready to become more independent to do so.

Ongoing individual, group, and family therapy is given by four full-time therapists and the therapy supervisor. The therapist needs to have a master's degree in social work or clinical psychology. Each girl, on arriving, is assigned a therapist who remains with her during the length of her stay. The therapist helps the girl develop a plan and a set of goals for herself over the period she remains. These goals may include better attendance at school, more control over personal behavior, or more self-confidence. Each girl's therapist works with her individually two times a week. The girls also participate in two group therapy sessions each week.

Whenver possible, we bring family members into the counseling process because they can be a tremendous help to the girl's efforts in therapy. Also, for many girls, family reunification is the best possible option if it can be done in a healthy, constructive way. Family members are involved in individual counseling as well as in cross-family groups that deal with common issues and problems.

The therapist also acts as a "case manager," keeping track of each girl's overall progress and making sure that her full range of needs are addressed (either from inside the agency or through outside agency resources). The therapist plays a central role in each girl's overall progress. She coordinates all aspects of the girl's treatment and schooling, assesses her needs and the degree to which they are being met, and assists her, at the appropriate time, to develop a plan for leaving and becoming more independent.

Most of the girls attend the accredited nonpublic special education high school located on-grounds. The high school is staffed by three full-time teachers and six full-time teacher's assistants, and provides highly individualized instruction. We emphasize allowing each student to reach her greatest potential. Our school director is highly regarded in the community as a dedicated and talented educator. Special enrichment activities include field trips, sewing, creative writing classes, and guest speakers.

Older girls who are preparing to leave the program take a special counseling and education course. The course aims to help the girls learn "living skills"—those needed to function independently in the community. These include how to comparison shop for groceries, how to plan a healthy diet, general health care, and finding and maintaining an apartment or other suitable living arrangement.

We have an exciting range of recreation and physical education activities that are coordinated by the recreation director. Aerobics, dance, ice skating, horseback riding, jogging, walking, and sports are regular offerings. There are also two to four outings each weekend to special locations, such as museums, parks, or the movies.

We favor a comprehensive, individualized approach, with a close therapeutic relationship at its core. We think this is necessary for young people who have experienced extreme damage during the early years of their lives.

Programs Serving Runaway and Homeless Youth

CASE IN POINT

(Practitioners Talk About Their Work with Clients)

ROGER

Our counseling center connects with young people at a time of severe crisis in their lives—many broken pieces need to be mended. There are numerous issues to be dealt with. The kids are homeless and laden with the effects of abandonment, demonstrated in their running away: criminality, lack of trust, low self-esteem, drug and alcohol involvement, school failure, prostitution, and so forth. I've seen it all.

These kids can be from anywhere and reflect many cultural, ethnic, and socioeconomic backgrounds. Physical size can also be a distinction; one of my girls is six-feet tall and another one is a dwarf, and so I have been exposed extensively to the "little" people culture.

Their needs, at one level, are very similar and very human: they all want understanding, love, information, guidance, and connection with community supportive services.

In the beginning, intimacy needs to be achieved quickly: a story needs to be told, and a plan needs to be constructed, including the changes that they want to make.

An example is Roger—sixteen-and-one-half years old upon first contact—a black male.

I first connected with Roger by phone at the shelter where he was residing. He was attempting to get back into the Job Corps (he had been kicked out for threatening another kid with a knife). I made an appointment to visit, and, upon my arrival, I was told that Roger had been expelled. He and his friend were moving to another shelter. Could I give them a ride? As I wasn't going to be in that area until later that afternoon, they had to agree to drive around with me for the day. It was Christmastime, and I was playing Santa and delivering gifts to the kids on my caseload all over town, and so we packed up my car with their worldly possessions and off we went.

I got to know Roger very well, quickly, driving around in the car that way. He had just come off the streets from a bout with drug sales and prostitution. He appeared serious and motivated about changing this way of life and making it on his own. He "hated" his Mom and unfolded a lengthy history of physical and emotional abuse, seeing himself as unloved and unwanted. It sounded very real and very destructive. We ended our day having a bite in a local cafe.

I found out about a new six-bed emancipation home where Roger could complete his schooling, work, receive therapy, and learn to live on his own. He interviewed and got in.

His mom visited with me and presented herself as dysfunctionally obese (she appeared to have difficulty breathing and walking) and complained about her son being "no good" and not understanding enough about all her illnesses. Furthermore, she blamed Roger's misbehavior and insolence for much of her physical state. A series of group sessions with Roger, a therapist, Roger's mom, and myself were very disquieting, to say the least. A good piece of time would be needed to heal all the wounds.

At the end of six months, Roger had taken on two jobs: during the day he worked for a well-known airline company in a modern high-rise; at night he worked in a fast-food joint. He decided to discontinue his schooling for a while so he could set aside some money and get away from the academic grind. A new place to live had to be found.

I had heard about a service organization offering an apartment with no first and last month payment required. Weekly counseling would be provided as well. Roger got accepted and moved in. Roger and I had a wonderful domestic moment together several months later when the living room furniture arrived.

Roger has reached eighteen years of age, and so his case is legally closed. He is still living in his apartment, working full-time for the airline, and has a talking relationship with his mom. He is making plans to return to school—by this time he has a strong desire to do that. I have been able to connect Roger up with an organization that assists young people to obtain grants to continue their education.

One of the best moments was several weeks ago when Roger arrived, completed tax forms in hand, requesting that I look them over. A new dimension of my job had come about; tax consultant!

This chapter synthesizes research on the evaluation of agency programs serving runaway and homeless youth. As before, generalizations are followed by action guidelines for policy development. Many of the available studies on programs overlap the period when runaways were under court jurisdiction, and included other types of status offenders. The findings are suggestive rather than precise with regard to runaways.

The task of reviewing and evaluating the existing literature was more vexing than it first appeared. Successful intervention programs were difficult to identify, because the available studies are weak, inconclusive, and contradictory. Analyses of programs are fragmented (Denno, 1980). Programs are geared to a variety of different youth populations, have different goals, and contain varying components, making comparisons difficult. There is variation in the length and intensity of treatment offered. With respect to their sponsorship, some programs are closely tied to the local policy department or court, some are provided by private or public agencies under court jurisdiction, while others are administered by completely independent agencies (Binder and Newkirk, 1977; Collingwood and Engelsgjerd, 1977; Collingwood, Williams, and Douds, 1976; Stollery, 1977). Program composition, staffing, funding, and complexity vary. Definitions of terms and research methodologies differ; there is not even the beginning of agreement on standardized methods. Some programs are carried out by agencies in an isolated fashion, whereas others have a great deal of interagency and community collaboration. The time period before follow-up program evaluation is irregular. It is not surprising, then, that a consensus does not readily emerge from the different studies.

Research into the effects of programs on the recidivism rates of status offenders has produced markedly mixed results (Labin, 1980). It has been argued that programs have no effect on recidivism (Bohnstedt, 1978; Smith, Bohnstedt, and Tompkins, 1979; Sorensen, 1978); dramatically reduce recidivism (Collingwood, Williams, and Douds, 1976; Gilbert, 1977); and slightly reduce recidivism (Palmer, 1979).

Negative assessments of status offender programs have been made on different bases. One is that these programs serve low-risk individuals and thus are merely a way for those who would otherwise be released to come under court control (Bohnstedt, 1978; Boisvert and Wells, 1980; Labin, 1980; Smith, Bohnstedt, and Tompkins, 1979). LaPlante (1977) suggests that many problems have been created by the presence of diversion programs. These include an increment in offenses resulting from a loss of the deterrent effect of punishment and, therefore, an increase in danger to the public. McCarthy (1981) argues that child welfare workers, responsible for status offenders as a result of the law transferring responsibility for adolescent status offenders from the juvenile justice system to the child welfare system, appear to be reluctant to intervene in cases that do not entail an obvious risk of abuse to youth. Therefore, the new law may, in fact, partially constitute a de facto experiment in "radical nonintervention."

Other researchers point out that many status offender programs operate in ways inconsistent with their original conceptualization. Larson and Roll (1977) argue that, although labeling theory represented one of the bases for diversion projects, those involved in providing such programs view them very differently. The programs are either thought of as diverting youth away from the juvenile justice system or are seen as a means for preventing young people from receiving needed services.

In this analysis of status offender programs, our approach has been to identify successful programs, that is, those that have attained their intended goals, based on explicit empirical research evidence and evaluation. Research procedures were not examined in depth. When evidence of success was presented by the researcher and there were no glaring deficiencies suggesting that the study be eliminated from our data pool, it was included in the analysis that follows. The term status offender is used to designate youth originally included in that category.

For a study to be included, it was necessary to isolate some specific program elements in the intervention investigated. In some instances, programs were so multidimensional and complex that it was impossible to determine which variables might have affected the results.

FAMILY-ORIENTED INTERVENTION

Generalization VI: Family-oriented counseling and therapy have been found to be effective intervention modes for working with status offenders (Baron and Feeney, 1973; Beal and Duckro, 1977; Binder and Newkirk, 1977; Bohnstedt, 1978; D'Angelo, 1984; Druckman, 1979; Gruher, 1979; Kelley, Schulman, and Lynch, 1976; Kogan, 1980; Michaels and Green, 1979; McAndrews, 1981; Morgan, 1982; Piven, 1979; Reilly, 1978; Stratton, 1975). (For Generalizations I–V, see Chapter 2.)

One of the strongest generalizations to emerge relates to the efficacy of family-oriented intervention in serving status offenders. The positive effects of family crisis therapy on recidivism are noted in the project evaluations of Baron and Feeney (1973) and Bohnstedt (1978). After nine months of operation, the Sacramento County 601 Diversion Project showed a decrease in the recidivism rate for juvenile status offenders (Baron and Feeney, 1973). A later examination of eleven California juvenile diversion projects found that only three actually reduced recidivism, and these utilized specialized family crisis counseling (Bohnstedt, 1978).

The decline in youth involvement with the justice system generally is another positive outcome for programs involving family crisis therapy. Beal and Duckro (1977) report that juveniles treated with a family therapy intervention strategy were referred to the court system significantly less often than a similar sample of nonprogram participants. McAndrews (1981) presents a case study of an outreach therapy program involving families with children and adolescents whose contact with the legal and social services systems results from status offenses. The findings show that short-term structural and strategic family therapy delivered in the homes of program participants is a promising alternative for those with previously unsatisfactory involvement with other mental health and human services.

From a more rigorous research standpoint, Stratton's (1975) study investigates whether specialized family crisis intervention shortly after initial police contact is more effective than traditional methods of dealing with status offenders and youthful misdemeanants. Among the traditional options are informal counseling, counseling with parents, the filing of a juvenile court petition, and immediate detention. Sixty subjects were randomly assigned to undergo either family crisis intervention or traditional approaches over a six-month period. At the conclusion of the study, the traditional and family crisis treatments were compared. The latter approach had a more favorable effect statistically on recidivism, on the use of probation department services, and on the number of days spent in detention at juvenile hall.

Several other studies highlight the usefulness of family involvement. Morgan's review (1982) of the literature indicates that the planning and implementation of programs for runaways must incorporate a family therapeutic approach—one sensitive to intergenerational forces like trust and loyalty. Reilly (1978) also recognizes the need for treatment measures that include the whole family. This research on runaway girls and their parents (involving psychiatric interviews, rating scales, and other psychotherapeutic data) points up the association between severe family disturbances and the dysfunctional behavior of status offenders.

Along these lines, Kogan (1980) reviewed the work of the Family Treatment Unit of the St. Louis County, Missouri, Juvenile Court. In an analysis of 52 status offender families referred to the unit, Kogan found above average indications of conflict. He concludes that putting parents effectively in control will result in favorable change for the child. This approach, he contends, represents the best means for changing dysfunctional family structure and minimizing family conflict. A New York study of youth classified as Persons in Need of Supervision (PINS) (Piven, 1979) is another example of the family focus. In a review of 187 cases of PINS appearing before the Manhattan Family Court, results shows that the majority were referred by their parents after unsatisfactory attempts had been made to address the multiple behavioral problems of their children. The findings suggest a need for voluntary intervention focusing on aid to troubled families experiencing serious behavior problems.

The significance of family intervention is dramatized in D'Angelo's study (1984) of a "one-shot" interview of families of runaways. In a structured experiment, he compared families who came for a single counseling interview with a control group who refused treatment. Families participating in the "one-shot" experience showed improvement in school adjustment of youth, parental self-confidence, and use of community resources. The researchers concluded that even the mildest form of family intervention in runaway situations increased the chances of conflict resolution and family cohesion.

Action Guideline VI: In working with runaways, family-oriented intervention should receive high priority. This mode of intervention can be geared toward achieving aims such as reducing recidivism (repeated episodes of running away), curtailing youth involvement with the juvenile justice system generally, aiding families that have not benefited from more traditional social service methods, fostering school adjustment among youth, enhancing parental self-confidence, encouraging more use of community resources by the family, and facilitating increased family cohesion. While no particular form of family therapy can, from the data, be identified as universally preferred, if resources are limited, even modest programs can have beneficial effects. Family therapy may effectively be applied by associating the program with the courts, by using law enforcement and outreach treatment in the home, employing short-term structured approaches, providing parents with behavior management skills, training youth in coping skills and appropriate behavior, and facilitating family communication. Family intervention may not be the best approach with all young people and in all situations. When families are extremely disorganized, where the environment is detrimental to youth (perhaps physical or sexual abuse is chronic), or where emancipation is the primary goal of the runaway, other approaches, including individual counseling and social support, may be employed. In all instances, however, family intervention should be seriously considered in the design of an intervention program.

USE OF VOLUNTEERS

Generalization VII: Using volunteers is an effective means of providing service to status offenders (Bauer et al., 1980; Blakely, 1981; Harris, 1982; Kelley, Kiyak, and Blak, 1979; Latina and Schembera, 1976; Mitchell, 1980; Quay and Love, 1977).

1. *College students have been found to be especially effective in working with status offenders* (Blakely, 1981; Mitchell, 1980).
2. *Volunteer performance is enhanced by proper training and supervision* (Bauer et al., 1980; Blakely, 1981; Mitchell, 1980).
3. *Placing status offenders with volunteer families in the community has produced beneficial results* (Latina and Schembera, 1976).

It is generally agreed that volunteer counselors are able to develop a close relationship with the client and to provide the individual attention necessary for effective treatment. Programs frequently offer many different kinds of services. Quay and Love (1977) considered one that provided vocational counseling, training and job placement, academic help on a tutorial and small-group basis, and personal and social counseling. Community volunteers worked in all areas of the program, particularly in academic counseling. Clients were young people between twelve and sixteen years of age adjudicated as delinquent, children designated in the need of supervision, and informally referred participants (those who had not entered the juvenile system). The program was successful in reducing recidivism rates, particularly among the informally referred youth. Other volunteer activities have included establishing close relationships with youth, and helping them to assess problem areas and to plan strategies for resolving their difficulties (Bauer et al., 1980). Other volunteers have used behavioral contracting to assess interpersonal difficulties and advocacy techniques to protect the rights of young people and to bring resources to bear to meet their needs.

The use of college student volunteers has been particularly positive in situations that call for intensely deliberate participation, such as working as a youth counselor (Mitchell, 1980; Bauer et al., 1980). In a comparative study of the contribution of unversity students, community college undergraduates, and other community volunteers to a juvenile diversion project, college volunteers were found to be willing to make a greater commitment of time and effort than other community members (Mitchell, 1980).

Studies by Bauer et al. (1980), Mitchell (1980), and Blakely (1981) included variables related to training and supervision of volunteers working with status offenders. These studies highlight the need to include appropriate training and supervision in any program designed to use volunteers.

In explaining the success of a deinstitutionalization pilot project in Tampa, Florida, Latina and Schembera (1976) noted the beneficial use of volunteer families for placement of status offenders. In their analysis of Florida detention patterns, they found that about 44 percent of the youth being detained in secure facilities required only temporary shelter and supervision. Under the program reviewed, such offenders were placed in the homes of volunteer families for no more than two weeks.

Action Guideline VII: Programs serving status offenders should consider the active use of volunteers. The volunteers may perform a wide variety of tasks: vocational counseling and placement, academic tutoring, personal and social counseling, establishing close relationships with youth, using behavioral contracting, and engaging in youth advocacy. College students can be especially effective in volunteer roles. They are close enough in age to have similar characteristics (as with peer counselors) but are experienced and educated enough to offer maturity and objectivity (as with professional counselors). In organizing a volunteer service program, care must be taken to incorporate well-formulated aspects of training and supervision in order to insure responsible service delivery. Volunteers should be encouraged to offer homes for placement purposes. Volunteers may also be used to good advantage, as conflict resolution mediators between youth and patients (see below).

USE OF COMMUNITY AGENCY RESOURCES

Generalization VIII: Effective programming for status offenders is associated with the use and cooperation of diverse community and agency resources (Binder and Newkirk, 1977; Boisvert, Kenney, and Kvaraceus, 1976; Handler and Zatz, 1982; McAndrews, 1981; Murray, 1982; Nelson, 1982; Polivka, Eccles, and Miller, 1979; Quay and Love, 1977; Spergel et al., 1982; Thomson and Treger, 1973; Young and Pappenfort, 1977). In the comprehensive National Academy of Science study of status offenders, Handler and Zatz (1982: 115) found that successful implementation of deinstitutionalization depends on "the availability of facilities at the local level—willing and able child welfare offices, group homes and shelter care, and other kinds of needed services." They added that the local community needs to have "the ability to coordinate and control" these various units which provide appropriate resources to troubled youth. In his extensive work on status offender research, Murray (1982: 36) states: "Clearly, there is no 'omnibus' status offender program but rather a variety of programs for a variety of needs. . . . What is needed is more diversity of approaches."

The cooperation of law enforcement with other agencies is noted in the program evaluations of Binder and Newkirk (1977) and Quay and Love (1977). Binder and Newkirk review the University of California, Irvine (UCI) Youth Services Program, a juvenile diversion project in which the police redirect minor offenders to community agencies for early counseling. The UCI Youth Services Program began in 1971 as a cooperative effort between the local police department and a university pilot internship project. By 1976 the program had become the police diversion component in a municipal consortium encompassing thirteen cities. The program counselors worked within police facilities in their efforts to redirect juvenile behavior. The evaluators concluded that cooperative interaction with other community units was conducive to the success of the UCI program.

McAndrews (1981) found that the beneficial consequences of an outreach family therapy program resulted from an expansion of available resources and an outcome of case-specific interagency collaboration. Focusing on how youth are assigned to secure detention or to a community-based alternative program, Young and Pappenfort (1977) examined four alternative formats (residential and nonresidential) and found the four to be roughly comparable in keeping both status offenders and alleged delinquents trouble free. The researchers concluded that communities need to develop diverse, flexible alternatives to secure detention for children in trouble.

Action Guideline VIII: Effective programming for status offenders requires that a community examine its local situation to determine whether there is a sufficient range of services to meet the needs of troubled youth. Where services are lacking or inadequate, they should be developed. Also, mechanisms should be established to promote coordination among the service providers in order to optimize the delivery of services to young people and to ensure that no needy youth "fall between the cracks." Such mechanisms may include regularly scheduled meetings of relevant agencies, specially constituted interagency study groups or task forces to deal with particular problems, a community newsletter, sharing of service statistics and agency reports, joint programs, formal client referral procedures, interagency relationship contracts, facility sharing, and temporary loaning or reassigning of staff.

RATIONAL INTAKE AND DISPOSITION PROCESSES

Generalization IX: Circumstances at the point of intake for entry into the service system can drastically affect the forms of treatment received by status offenders. Decisions about disposition and service modalities appear often to be based on irrelevant, discriminatory, or nondiagnostic considerations. Intake decisions are influenced by such stereotypic factors as race and ethnicity, class, gender, and presence of a parent or lawyer (Chambers, Grinnell, and Gorsuch, 1980; Clarke and Koch, 1980; Geller, 1981; Hayeslip, 1979; Heck, 1980; Hough, 1977; Lewis and Hess, 1981; Mann, 1976, 1979, 1980; Sundeen, 1974).

A concern of many researchers has been the processing response to status offenders and their families based on personal characteristics. Some studies confirm a widely held belief that decisions concerning status offenders are directly affected by the personal attributes of the offender such as race, sex, dress, and demeanor. Specifically, it has been claimed that the dress and demeanor of black adolescent offenders contribute to more severe treatment and that urban youth become more deeply involved in the juvenile justice system than rural youth (Lewis and Hess, 1981; Mann, 1976, 1979). Following intensive observation of one judge, Mann (1980) concluded that *his* disposition were not influenced by such extraneous factors. This is explained by Lewis and Hess (1981) in terms of philosophical differences among judges. Thus, individual predilections on the part of intake personnel also unpredictably affect the fate of status offenders.

The sex of a status offender appears to correlate with different patterns of treatment. More males than females are charged by the police, while more females than males are charged by school board officials for truancy and by parents for being incorrigible and running away. Also, streaming by sex exists within the criminal justice and psychiatric systems (Geller, 1981; Mann, 1976, 1979). Research suggests that females receive more severe dispositions for person offenses, are held in custody longer, and are allocated less average time for their disposition than males (Mann, 1976). Although they commit less serious offenses, more females are held in detention than males (31 percent versus 24 percent). Both the court and the police explain this discrepancy by claiming that females require protection for their safety and well-being (Kratcoski, 1974).

Evidence also suggests an implicit, and sexist, assumption concerning the sexual behavior of males and females. A young female's sexual involvement is taken to indicate self-destructiveness and the existence of personal, family, and emotional problems. Male heterosexual behavior is not viewed this way and is not taken as seriously. Typically, male behavior is defined as antisocial, the aggressive acting out of a male in conflict with his society. As a result of these different explanations of behavior, females are more likely to be given an out-of-home placement, whereas males are more likely to be allowed to remain in their own homes. Males are, proportionately, less likely to be placed in detention than females and more likely to be put on probation (Geller, 1981; Lewis and Hess, 1981). Hence, adolescent females who exhibit behavior inconsistent with their socialized and expected roles are more likely than males to be punished in juvenile court for transgressing sex role expectations (Mann, 1979).

Sex role stereotyping is further complicated by ethnicity. Mann (1976, 1979) found that black female runaways are often given more severe sanctions than black male runaways, and white male runaways are more harshly treated than white and nonwhite female runaways. Datesman and Scarpitti (1975) found that this double standard, while existing for white juveniles, is much less apparent for black adolescents.

Chambers, Grinnell, and Gorsuch (1980) indicate that older and black youth are likely to receive relatively harsher treatment. In their study of the discretionary process operating in a Texas county juvenile justice system, they found that the youthful offenders released to parents were likely to be younger and/or without prior official contacts with the police department. The juveniles referred to the county probation department by the police were more likely to be older and/or black; and, at the probation department stage, those more likely to be counseled and released were young and female.

It has been determined that the disposition decision is affected by the presence of either parent. If a parent is present, the minor runaway is more frequently accorded the least severe court disposition (Mann, 1979), and it appears that parents are more likely to appear in court on behalf of their sons than their daughters, and substantially more fathers appear for their sons (Mann, 1976). The court seems to react negatively when juveniles are represented by an attorney, irrespective of the type of counsel—private or court appointed (Clarke and Koch, 1980). Juveniles represented by an attorney are more likely to be committed to an institutional setting (Clarke and Koch, 1980; Hayeslip, 1979).

A study of forty-three Los Angeles police juvenile bureaus (Sundeen, 1974) highlights the complexities of decision making for status offenders. The findings indicate that decisions were affected by a combination of offender, police, and community characteristics. Among the most important influences was the background of the police officer making the disposition decision (amount of juvenile training received, extent of local friendships, and place of residence).

Action Guideline IX: In order to establish a rational, client-centered service delivery system for status offenders, special effort should be made to structure a point of entry situation that exhibits sound professional characteristics. Staff need to possess skills and attitudes allowing use of competency-based diagnostic techniques for making disposition decisions. These decisions may relate to service provided to clients either directly or through referral to a range of appropriate community resources. Staff should be expected to make disposition decisions without relying on stereotypic factors, such as race, ethnicity, class, or sex. Currently, youth are frequently streamed according to which of many different agencies and organizations they happen to stumble upon. They have been identified, often in a haphazard fashion, as abused and neglected youth, juvenile status offenders, or juvenile criminal offenders.

USE OF COMPETENT STAFF

Generalization X: Use of competent, well-trained staff is associated with effective and cost efficient service delivery to status offenders. Some important skills that have been identified include recognizing conflicting perspectives, resolving conflicts among different parties, knowing about organizational context effects, engaging in productive interagency collaboration, defining a proper role for oneself, employing both adversarial and nonadversarial techniques differentially, and using authority appropriately.

In a study of juvenile correctional programs conducted for the California State Assembly, Greenwood (1982) concluded that the main variable associated with program effectiveness was the character of the staff. Cost effectiveness factors were examined in a comparative study of York County, Pennsylvania, status offenders who received family therapy and a control group who did not (Michaels and Green, 1979). A savings of more than $78,000 over a two-year period resulted from cost reductions associated with having trained child welfare workers to intervene in the family situation of status offenders, instead of placing the youth outside their own homes.

The detrimental effects of inadequate staff have also been examined. In reviewing ways to improve services for youthful offenders in the fifteen east Tennessee counties surrounding Knoxville, Bolton and Brown (1978) surveyed personnel from law enforcement, the judiciary, and counseling services and learned that offenses among younger age groups were becoming more common in the rural environment. The researchers reported that, along with the problems of funding and gaining public acceptance of new ideas, the shortage of qualified staff, particularly in rural areas, was a major obstacle to improving youth services. In the contrasting urban context of Washington, D.C., Chapin's (1978) investigation of runaway youth drawn into prostitution points up similar staffing concerns. In this case, the unsuccessful efforts of a local church to establish a pilot shelter program of counseling and health services were attributed in part to staffing problems; there was clearly a need for trained staff able to supervise a referral system, provide counseling, and manage an outreach program that would contact runaways at local transportation centers before they became caught up in the prostitution web.

A number of significant skills required of staff have been identified. Among these is the ability to recognize the conflicting views of relevant parties. Murphy (1983) used situational analysis of actors and perspectives at play to show that the perspectives of parents and youth are frequently in conflict with those of the professionals working with them. This potential clash of views is noted as well in Daley's (1983) survey of social workers who served as case advocates in the detention hearing process. The study's major findings indicate that this advocacy process works differently for parents and probation workers, with effective advocacy taking place in cases where conflict among the parties is kept to a minimum.

Lewis and Hess (1981) focus on key factors associated with judicial decision making in Alabama, where the treatment of status offenders was legally differentiated from that of delinquent youth. On the basis of findings that suggest complete deinstitutionalization of status offenders, with such youth being served in open, community-based facilities, the researchers conclude that social service agencies must have personnel who understand the nature and extent of court authority and how to use it. This is reflected essentially in close and continuous collaboration between agency staff and the court.

Duryee (1980) emphasizes the interrelationship among content, method, and optimal setting for training family therapists in an interethnic status offender service agency. The atmosphere of questioning provided by the emphasis on training kept the agency staff continually aware of its nonadversarial role. Thus, while working side by side with the adversarial model of the juvenile justice system, staffers recognized that the agency's role was to eliminate effectively just such aspects from family relationships. In a related study of decision making in a Pennsylvania child welfare agency, which had taken over status offender responsibility from the juvenile justice system, McCarthy (1981) confirmed a prediction that agency staff would rely on traditional orientations of the child welfare system in making service decisions. In a thematic analysis of 180 agency case records, the study noted that case workers appeared reluctant to intervene where there was no obvious risk of abuse to youth, promoting a form of service neglect or abuse through radical nonintervention.

Action Guideline X: Organizations established to provide community based services should engage competent, well-qualified staff. The staff should have the ability to recognize conflicting perspectives, resolve conflicts among different parties, know about organizational context effects, engage in productive inter-agency collaboration, define a proper role for themselves, employ both adversarial and nonadversarial techniques differentially, and use authority appropriately. The staff should also be firmly grounded in the psychology and problems of adolescent youth. A competent staff can be assembled through careful recruitment or well-formulated, sustained training and development programs.

SPECIFIC EFFECTIVE PROGRAM APPROACHES

Generalization XI: A variety of specific program approaches have been associated with effective service delivery. Successful programs include the following: mediation between adolescents and parents; individually tailored approaches using varied community resources; limiting the range of services provided by the agency; vocational counseling; academic tutoring; physical fitness opportunities; advocacy programming; and combinations of two or more program components. No single approach has received widespread support in the research literature (Abbott and Blake, 1988; Clark, Ringwalt, and Ciminello, 1985; Collingwood and Engelsgjerd, 1977; Collingwood, Williams, and Douds, 1976; Heck, 1980; Kelley, Schulman, and Lynch, 1976; Mitchell, 1980; Murray, 1982; Quay and Love, 1977).

A Wayne County, Michigan, juvenile diversion program that seeks to prevent recidivism and minimize justice system penetration places its participants in individually tailored multimodel treatment plans (Kelley, Shulman, and Lynch, 1976). Accordingly, existing community services, youth service center resources, and counseling services of both a direct individual and family type are variously combined, depending on the client's special needs. Among the desirable outcomes noted for the treatment group over the control group were significantly fewer official contacts with the court, fewer officially adjudicated delinquents, and few institutional commitments.

Results from a study adopting an extremely broad perspective suggest that recidivism among runaways can best be explained by the structure of programs within the facilities through which youth move. Those with a wide range of services showed increased recidivism of status offenders, while facilities that effectively focus on a limited range of services had lower recidivism rates for five different types of offense (Heck, 1980).

The importance of environmentally oriented support was shown in a study conducted by Quay and Love (1977). A program featuring vocational counseling, vocational training, academic counseling, and tutoring was particularly successful in reducing recidivism rates.

The Youth Section of the Dallas, Texas, police force instituted a program that emphasized physical fitness. During the first two months, offenders received training in physical, emotional, and intellectual skills. During the next four months, intellectual and emotional skills were stressed and the young people engaged in a recreational activity of individual choice. The participants in the program showed an increase in fitness during the first year of 12 percent, as measured by tests of the American Association for Health, Physical Education and Recreation. After the set program, approximately 50 percent continued to participate voluntarily. Compared to a Bose recidivism rate of 35 percent, these youth had a 2.7 percent rearrest rate. The program combined physical fitness with emotional and intellectual components (Collingwood and Engelsgjerd, 1977; Collingwood, Williams, and Douds, 1976).

Mitchell (1980) reports on a juvenile diversion program that combines advocacy with behavioral contracting. With respect to advocacy, the requisite resources are located and created. Behavioral contracting emphasizes the specific interpersonal circumstances that exist for a youth and his or her significant others. A positive impact on the recidivist behavior of participating youth was noted. As in the previous example of vocational skill training, a single dimension approach was avoided. Effective programs seem to combine several components in a synchronized design.

While it is possible to point to program success in diverse situations, no universally authenticated program strategies emerge in the evaluation research. As Clarke, Ringwalt, and Ciminello (1985: 27) state, after a comprehensive review of available empirical findings, "there is no substantial accumulation of evidence to support the efficacy of any treatment or service." Murray, after a similar investigation (1982: 36), arrives at the conclusion previously mentioned on page 53 of this text.

Action Guideline XI: Organizations wishing to adopt effective program approaches might consider the following as possibilities: a mediation service to resolve differences between teenagers and their parents; vocational counseling and job placement services; academic tutoring; physical fitness and recreation opportunities; and advocacy activities. It is useful to tailor a mix of programs for specific individuals, making use of various agency and community resources. Combining program approaches is likely to increase service impact. A planning or service agency should also consider narrowing the scope of problem components and the target population to avoid spreading itself too thin. This also encourages targeting high-priority client groups and developing the competency and experience to do quality work.

TRUANCY PROGRAMS

Generalization XII: Truancy has been reduced through differing techniques: early identification of truancy-prone students through a detailed predictive profile; use of intrusive, coercive influence methods; and more traditional helping methods (Grala and McCauley, 1976; Miller, 1981; Murphy, 1983; Saccuzzo and Milligan, 1973).

Miller (1981) describes how the Allentown, Pennsylvania, School District employs the *early identification* technique to determine the characteristics of truancy at various levels. According to the research, the truant has self-perceptions of societal estrangement and has experienced low self-esteem and negative labeling by school, parents, and peers; demographically, the truant is likely to be fifteen or sixteen years old, to belong to a family in which both parents are employed, and to have repeated a grade. The last factor is supported by Murphy's (1983) study of the situational sets of significant actors in the juvenile justice system. He found that most youthful offenders, including truants, have school troubles.

When thirty-two chronic truants from a low-income, inner-city Philadelphia area received counseling that involved truant appeal, it was sufficient to change their intention to return to school (actual school attendance required further supportive instruction) (Grala and McCauley, 1976).

Favorable change in behavior of truants was reported by more than 80 percent of the 150 parents and children attending a single mass truancy hearing in court, scheduled with appropriate legal notice to all parties and featuring remarks from a significant person in the community (Saccuzzo and Milligan, 1973).

Success with truants has not been limited to coercive intervention methods. Group counseling techniques (Kahn, Lewis, and Galvez, 1974; Nagle et al., 1979), as well as contingency contracting (Nagle et al., 1979), have been highly rated.

Action Guideline XII: To curtail truancy, it is useful to identify early those students who are prone to absentee behavior. A profile of the potential truant includes such factors as self-perception of societal estrangement, low self-esteem, and negative labeling by the school, parents, and peers. The potential truant is likely to be fifteen or sixteen years of age, to belong to a family in which both parents are employed, and to have repeated a grade in school. It would be useful to consider intrusive and coercive intervention techniques, such as threat, appeal, counseling, or a mass truancy hearing in court. More traditional helping interventions, such as group counseling and contingency contracting, have also been effective with some truants. It is wise to consider alternative approaches in a combined intervention package or to determine which type of approach would be best for particular groups of students.

These last chapters have relied on existing research knowledge to inform the design of interventions for status offenders. Chapter 4 focuses on observations and opinions of knowledgeable experts in Los Angeles County, California, to pursue the analysis of the status offender problem at the local level and for recommendations of appropriate corrective action. Policy initiatives provided in Chapter 5 draw on these two varied but related sources of knowledge on the subject.

GETTING ORGANIZED

(Administrators Talk About Their Agencies)

THE TEMP-LODG PROGRAM

When it comes to developing a program to serve the needs of the community, it's important to be especially sensitive to what that community is and how the design of your program can be most helpful. Temp-Lodg (Temporary Lodging) started in the early 1970s in a county that is used as a pass-through area between two large cities. Our county has a population of about 600,000 in a rather extended geographic region—a mix of suburban and rural districts. There were very few social services in the county at that time and absolutely no shelter programs or services for runaway or homeless youth in crisis. But we have a growing problem, because kids were passing between the two big towns and many noticed that our peaceful and really beautiful county is an appealing place to stop off.

The county began looking toward developing what was then the most prominent model of serving these youth, a group shelter, "crash pad"—or whatever you want to call it—but we realized that many young people could never physically get to those services if we established one central house. Also, we started looking at the different areas where we could put this house. And everyone said, "It's needed, but not here, please!" So we realized we had to go a bit underground to solve this problem, and we developed the "Temp-Lodg" model.

This is a decentralized system of licensed volunteer foster homes. We recruit the volunteers, train the foster parents, and provide reimbursement. We have a partnership with the county, which does initial licensing for the homes. The Temp-Lodge program operates under strict standards, even though it is a volunteer and short-term operation. All families receive an unannounced visit four months after receiving the license and once a year after that. A summary inspection notice is officially filed by the county after each such visit.

The program has become extremely successful because it is both cost-effective and doesn't burn people out. All of us in this field recognize that we start out with great enthusiasm, but if you're, in fact, having to be that 2 o'clock-in-the-morning staff member dealing with problems, you eventually can get disillusioned and wear down. The Temp-Lodg families are volunteer community people who are asked for brief but intense involvements. Then they can take time off and come back rejuvenated. Our families are reimbursed $10 for every night they have a child in their home.

Originally, we had many families in which mothers didn't work, and so the foster families were able to provide twenty-four-hour care. Now we have fewer and fewer families in which that occurs, so we devised a new system. We go out and pick the kids up at the family site every morning and bring them into our day program, which has tutors and medical care, group counseling, and drug-alcohol counseling. Then we take the children back to the lodge homes in the evening, about 5 or 6 o'clock. In this way, round-the-clock supervision is assured. The staff is responsible for the kids during the work week, and the Temp-Lodg parents are there for them on evenings and weekends. The kids stay with us a maximum of thirty days, but we're actually averaging just under a week.

Youth are matched to homes on the basis of availability, geographic location, and, most important, the suitability of the family in terms of being able to provide a supportive experience for that particular kid. The program at any one time has about 25 licensed homes spread throughout the county. All transportation for school, medical needs, psychological testing, counseling, and Monday through Friday supervision and recreation is provided by the program.

About 75 percent of our kids do go back home. The others don't but are brought before an interagency case council made up of the key planners for each of our county departments. Temp-Lodg is the only private agency that sits on that. The council was started because so many of the kids were passed on between departments because staff didn't want to take them. We would bring the kid over to protective services, and they'd say, "No, we can't accept that kid," so we'd take him back to probation, and they'd say no also. The agreement now is that any child brought before the interagency case council *will not leave the room* until it has been decided who will handle the case and how. There is much better cooperation, and the concept is fully supported by the county board of supervisors.

This Temp-Lodg model does work, and what's meaningful from our standpoint is that it actively involves citizens in responding to an important community problem. The volunteer families have been enthusiastic and are telling the story of the program to their church groups and civic associations.

CHAPTER 4

A Reflection of
the National Problem:
The Los Angeles Scene

CASE IN POINT

(Practitioners Talk About Their Work with Clients)

ROSA

With Rosa it was like swimming upstream the whole time. She was fifteen years old when I first met her three years ago, but she looked maybe eighteen or nineteen. She had been referred to our office at City Youth Guidance by a temporary shelter program specializing in outreach to hard-core street kids. Rosa had been prostituting for two years already and wanted out. She was looking for a long-term residential situation that would help her find a new direction for her life. That's what she came in asking for.

Our office was just starting up at the time, and we were assigning workers on a random basis to kids as they made contact. She might have done better with a female counselor, but we had no clear evidence then, or now, on what is the best arrangement for matching up staff with clients.

I got a quick rundown from Rosa on her situation and gathered additional information in conferences over a period of several months. It was obviously painful for her to recount her background, and I admit it wasn't a casual thing for me to hear about it either. The case history told of a series of awesome experiences that it must have been tough for a young child to cope with.

Rosa's troubles began a long time ago, in Mexico, before she was born. Her mother, let's call her Maria, had had two out-of-wedlock daughters, both by different men. The younger was ten years older than Rosa. Rosa was also an out-of-wedlock child by another man, but Maria married two years later for the first time, bringing a stepfather into the picture.

The stepfather was obviously less than exemplary, as Maria's family wanted nothing to do with him and invited them to stay away. The couple decided to make a new life for themselves in the United States, wanting to leave the three children behind. The grandparents were willing to keep the older children but insisted that Maria take the young baby with her. That's how Rosa made her way here.

Growing up in this family in the states was more the unfolding of a nightmare than the fulfillment of a dream. Rosa told me that her stepfather molested her sexually for as far back as she could remember. In addition to this, he was a severe alcoholic, which led to a liver condition that killed him when Rosa was eight.

Her mother was no help at all in this. Rosa described her as emotionally unstable, a steady drinker, depressed, and a constant source of put-downs: "She never took any responsibility or cared after me." When the girl complained of sexual abuse, Maria became agitated and insisted she was making it up. Rosa stated her mother believed everything her stepfather said up until his death. In addition, Maria blamed Rosa for hastening his death by defying him. From recurrent discussions with Rosa and with her mother, I believe this presents an accurate picture of the circumstances.

Rosa characterized her life as miserable, and she began to stay away from home and find companionship on the streets. When she was fourteen, an older boy, about twenty, befriended her, took her into his place, and over a period of time gradually induced her to engage in sex with other men so that they would have enough money to live on. This went on until her visit to our agency.

Rosa told me she hadn't seen her mother for three years, so I traced her, with Rosa's consent, and made a visit. I immediately was subjected to a diatribe about Rosa—she was a liar, she stole, frustrated her stepfather who was trying to be good to her, and aggravated his illness. Maria blamed the girl for almost everything bad that happened, complaining that she had "messed up my life." Maria didn't speak English well, but I understood her well enough, especially since these points were made with such emphasis. I came to agree with Rosa that her mother was, at least to some degree, mentally ill.

The mother consented to my plan to arrange a placement for Rosa in a residential program. Rosa and I visited several group homes together. She didn't want a foster situation. At my suggestion, she agreed to Lambert House, a comprehensive facility with a very strong therapy component. I had some agency funds available to assure her a room right away. The facility also had a school on site, which I thought was important for her.

The arrangement started out well enough. Her therapist told me that Rosa was holding back in treatment, but she was doing excellent work in her studies. Although she was below grade level, she seemed intelligent and was receiving good marks.

Two months later Rosa called me to say she was back on the streets. There were too many rules at the place, her freedom was being restricted, and she had gotten into a relationship with a guy who encouraged her to leave. This was to be only one of a series of relationships with exploiting males. In our talks, Rosa stated that she didn't want to go back to Lambert House, although she was continuing to have contact with her therapist. She now felt a foster home would be more like a family situation, and she wanted that. I was able to make arrangements with a highly experienced foster mother who liked the challenge of working with difficult young people. The placement was arranged, again with her mother's approval, and provision was made for Rosa to attend a special school for youth having emotional problems. My contacts with Rosa suggested that the extra support of this kind of school would be necessary to keep her attending class.

I called her attention to the exploitative relationships she was getting into with men and pointed to the possibility that they were a continuation of the early experiences with her father. I tried to draw her out and have her ventilate about this. Rosa acknowledged this pattern blankly and then entered into the next relationship. My continuing efforts to have her come to grips with this issue failed to hit the mark.

I kept in periodic touch with both Rosa and the foster parent by telephone, occasionally making suggestions about minor problems that came up. After six months, I received a call from the foster mother saying that Rosa was gone. She had hooked up with another boyfriend and had been staying out late at night. The other kids let on that the boyfriend was a pusher and Rosa was on drugs. The foster mother had put her on probation for a month in an attempt to control her movements outside of the home. Rosa wouldn't accept this and left. Where to was unknown.

After another month, Rosa herself called me. The boyfriend had put her out, and she had no place to go. She also spoke of needing help with a drug problem. I was able to locate a teen residence that also conducted an intensive substance abuse program. It was out at the fringe of the city and served thirty clients, all girls. Some of my previous clients had had good luck there. But the same scenario followed. Rosa met another guy and went off with him.

When Rosa called me three months later, it was not only to make contact but also to let me know she was pregnant. She had split up with her boyfriend, her mother wouldn't let her come in with her, and she wanted to keep the baby. Where could she go? I referred her to a highly professional maternity program I knew of for unwed Hispanic girls. I urged her to take full advantage of the counseling they offered about decisions on keeping the child and preparing for the period after birth. I kept in close touch with her during this time. She decided to go ahead with her wish to keep the child and would return to live with the father. I mainly encouraged her to work closely with the specialized counselors and supported her in her decisions. I hoped that she would now move into a more stable circumstance.

In my next follow-up call to her, I learned that the boyfriend had stolen a car and was sent to prison. Rosa was living with his sister, who was also providing the basic care for the child. Rosa asked me to visit her there and see the baby. We spent a pleasant hour, with me entertaining the cheerful, handsome, tiny fellow with my keys and by clicking noises with my tongue, while Rosa puttered about serving me cookies and coffee. We talked informally about her current arrangement, plans to work part-time, need to be more independent with men, and so on.

When I last called her sister-in-law's number, I learned that Rosa had left and was back on the streets. The baby had been put into protective custody. Nobody knew how to reach Rosa. It has been a year since I've heard anything from her.

Rosa was one of my most difficult and draining cases. I can't mark it off as a success. Over the entire period, I don't believe I was really able to establish a genuine, working relationship. She always held a part of herself back, in a kind of friendly disengagement. Throughout, she continued always to want to connect with her mother and her mother continued always to reject her overtly. That block in relating has probably generalized and affects her ability to get close to other people.

I threw an awful lot of help at her, but there wasn't enough of Rosa there to receive it. Someone once used the term "the walking wounded." That's the way I think about her. I was able to give her some comfort and get her over some rough spots. But life had inflicted some terrible wounds on her in her early years—and afterward—that I think maybe were too serious for anyone to heal.

Los Angeles has been viewed by many informed observers as the runaway capital of the nation. Together with New York and Florida, it is a beacon, drawing in bored, adventurous, lonely, dispirited young people seeking a haven. Runaways are attracted by the glamor of Hollywood, the allure of sandy beaches, and the benign climate. The situation in Los Angeles, for these reasons, both reflects aspects of the general subject and, in some ways, signals the cutting-edge developments in coping with the problem of runaway and homeless youth.

A structured community survey was conducted to obtain the observations and opinions of experts in Los Angeles County about runaways, homeless youth, and other status offenders. In addition, eight runaways were seen in two different shelters. The knowledgeable individuals who were interviewed included agency personnel who run short-term shelters, group homes, and residential treatment facilities; providers of outreach services, health services, and hot-line counseling; Probation Department officers and administrators; judges; law enforcement officials; school district personnel; and Department of Children's Services (DCS) staff. The results encompass the informed opinions of all those—including the runaways themselves—who are most qualified to represent the community's wisdom about status offenders. Thirty-four experts participated, who were related to twenty-nine organizations, fourteen of which provided direct services to runaways. Most of the discussion summarizes the replies of the experts, except when responses by runaways are specifically indicated.

See Appendix A for a complete discussion and description of the survey methodology, Appendix B for the questionnaire utilized, and Appendix C for a list of the people who were interviewed.

The findings of the survey are reported here in four sections: (1) the population and the problem; (2) current programs and services; (3) key issues; and (4) respondents' policy and program recommendations. Policy-oriented readers may wish to proceed immediately to the last section, although policy recommendations by the respondents can best be understood and evaluated in the context of needs and the resources now available to meet them. Furthermore, policy implications are found in all the sections.

Each of the four sections deals with answers to the items in the questionnaire, but not necessarily with all of them or in the order asked. The presentation of survey data is structured according to topic. A statement, in boldface type, summarizes the questionnaire responses. Detail, discussion, and quotations follow. Different numbers of individuals or agencies responded to each question.

The study describes the point in time when it was conducted in 1985. Since then the situation has changed in a favorable direction. A new local program was established through funds provided by state legislation, aimed at upgrading the degree of interagency planning and coordination for homeless youth. Also, a special service program for runaways was instituted by the Department of Children's Services (DCS) as a direct result of this study. Thus, some of the concerns that were expressed anticipating DCS reluctance to engage this population have been set to rest. This presentation, therefore, projects a snapshot of the situation as it existed a few years ago, and which likely reflects other communities that have not had similar support through their state legislatures.

The survey results should be viewed as suggestive and heuristic. It is a highly qualitative inquiry that draws together opinions of a group of well-informed community people. The data present not direct research observations of runaway and homeless youth but the considered views of individuals who have been intimately involved with these young people. These "soft" data are an interesting counterpart to the "hard" findings of the empirical research synthesis in the previous chapters. The survey data provide detail and vivid description that supplement the empirical material. They are of greatest use when they coincide with or reinforce the empirical material, as will be shown in the concluding chapter.

THE POPULATION AND THE PROBLEM

Changes in the Character of the Population

Respondents interviewed during the study believe the status offender population has become younger, with more ethnic representation (especially Hispanic), seemingly more abused and emotionally disturbed, probably composed of more youth from increasingly dysfunctional families, and possibly more female.

Professionals in the field often speculate about changes in the kinds of youth they are seeing. In response to a question on this topic, those interviewed gave these answers.

Changes Cited	Number of Respondents
Younger	11
More minorities	10
More Hispanics	6
More Asians	2
More blacks	2
More emotionally disturbed	7
More abused youth	7
Physical	4
Sexual	2
Other	1
More dysfunctional families	6
More females	4
More youth with complex problems	2
More youth with school problems	2
More homeless youth	2
More illegal aliens	2
Older youth	2
More substance-abuse problems	1
More middle-class youth	1
Fewer status offenders	1

These figures suggest six potential changes that deserve comment.

1. Eleven respondents reported that the population now being served is younger. Six respondents focused specifically on the range of ages. One shelter agency interviewee noted: "We definitely are getting some younger children. Twelve is not uncommon and occasionally an eleven-year-old." Another shelter agency respondent said that nine years ago "the majority [served] were fifteen and older. . . . Now we are getting eleven- and twelve-year-olds and our majority seems to be thirteen to fifteen." Other local experts have encountered even younger children—some nine- and ten-year-olds and others, "five- and six-year-olds even." School officials especially concerned with truancy offenses mentioned these early truancies and attributed them to neglect or unwitting subsidy of parents.

Other respondents discussed characteristics of the younger population. One pointed out: "It's a younger population, manifesting the same problems, the same behavior as the older kids." Another notes, "601s [truants] are younger with the age dropping for more serious offenses." Among the specific concerns raised were the increased use of drugs and alcohol among younger youth; the media's glorification of the runaway, so that the "sanction is disappearing from running away"; and kids getting "involved in problems at an early age but not getting treatment until they are older." According to this interviewee, "They don't get treatment until someone is brave enough to report the parents for neglect or the child commits a crime."

2. A second significant change is the increase in minority youth, especially Hispanic immigrants. Of the ten responses citing an increase in ethnic minorities, six mentioned the Hispanic or Spanish-speaking population. Comments focused on Hispanic immigrants, with one runaway shelter agency finding "a few more kids from Mexico and Central America—from zero to five each month" and another agency respondent noting "the cultural clash between generations" being experienced by immigrant youth who "feel freer now to leave home." This conflict was viewed from the parental perspective by another respondent, who notes the Hispanic parents' "reluctance to admit their failure at being *good* parents." Another respondent pointed out that, although "80 percent of the 500,000+ kids in the Los Angeles Unified School District are black or Hispanic, the problems of status offenders are not ethnically based."

3. Another third (seven of twenty-two) of the respondents report working with more emotionally disturbed children nowadays. Some noted that youth seem "more damaged," "more disturbed," "more desperate now." Others acknowledge generally that "kids are acting up" and displaying more "disruptive behavior," particularly in school. One agency representative emphasized that "before 1977, we saw mainly naughty kids who needed structure more than therapy"; now they are more in need of treatment.

4. A fourth change mentioned by seven of twenty-two interviewees is an increase in child abuse experienced by the youth population. One agency respondent reported that "child abuse has increased 25 percent in three years." Among this particular group of interviewees, four referred to a greater incidence of physical abuse. For one thing, "There is an increase in intensity in the home," and for another, there are "more assaults at a younger age." Consequently, as another respondent noted, "the awareness of physical and sexual abuse is increasing." Others among the seven in this group of respondents pointed to the increase in sexual abuse, as well as in child neglect.

5. Six interviewees remarked on a larger number of children from dysfunctional families. There are more problems with parents: "More kids are running as a solution to the increasing number of dysfunctional families." Most respondents focused on the parents' problems and their effect on the children. For some, "The family system seems significantly more disturbed . . . ," with parents "acknowledging their problems at an earlier age." Other respondents saw parents as "self-centered, self-absorbed and not connected with their kids," so that "parents are leaving younger kids." As another put it, "Nowadays parents just think about themselves: 'I don't need this, good-bye,' " leaving children to "accumulate on the streets." More sympathetically, another respondent said, "Parents . . . are often in crisis, too." Others cited basic structural issues in the family. Economic problems among parents contribute to difficulties, with a high AFDC (Aid to Families with Dependent Children) concentration among the truant population and an increase in single-parent households. As one school respondent said, "The family foundation upon which compulsory education is based no longer predominates and parents no longer value education."

6. Four of the respondents noted an increase in females served. One respondent said that "more teenage girls are 'hooking' in the [San Fernando] Valley now."

However, despite these perceived changes, some agencies say that their clientele remains the same. For one in particular, the "runaways still seem to be in the fourteen- to sixteen-year age bracket."

Refusal of Services to Runaways

Only four agencies claimed that they provide service to every youth who comes in the door. Others have varied reasons for refusing to give service but usually refer a client to a more appropriate service and even sometimes provide transportation.

The survey sought to learn whether youth arc generally being served when they approach agencies or whether they are being turned away for one reason or another. The survey also requested information on the reasons for refusal of service. An analysis of the agency responses provides some assessment of how the demand for services matches up with the supply of services available.

Of fourteen agencies that provide direct services and that responded to this question, four stated that they withheld services from no youth who requested assistance. Among the other ten, there was a range of turn-downs, with the highest yearly figure being 325 and the mean, 91. The ten agencies in this sample that indicated that they had rejected requests for services reported a total of 1,278 turn-downs for the year. So that this figure will not be misleading, it should be noted that any single youth may have been turned down by several different agencies; therefore, this figure does not indicate the number of clients rejected in a year.

Among the agencies responding to the survey, the reasons given for refusal of service were lack of beds, inappropriate agency (see further explanation in the next paragraph); substance abuse (youth high or intoxicated); and "miscellaneous" reasons, which included youth possessing a weapon, youth seeking to hustle or deal drugs, or youth refusing service by failing to give sufficient personal information.

Under "inappropriate agency," replies were further broken down into the following reasons: that the service needed was not available (long-term care, hospitalization); that the facility was unable to handle (suicidal, psychotic); that the agency accepted referrals from only one main source—the police.

Among the staff operating shelters, lack of available beds was the most common reason for turning a youth away. Respondents also stated that they did not serve youth who were referred inappropriately, for example children needing long-term care, hospitalization, or exhibiting psychotic or suicidal tendencies. Youth entering the agency in a chemically altered state are turned away to "cool out" and are encouraged to return when they have "come down."

Push-outs and Throwaway Youth

Runaways were once considered mainly youngsters who "skipped out" on their own. Recently, it has been recognized that parents are playing a large part in allowing, encouraging, or coercing the breakaway process. Almost half of the clientele seen by Los Angeles County agencies are reported to be in the push-out or throwaway category.

There is a considerable interest in whether detached young people have left home on their own volition or whether they have been compelled to leave by their parents. The Los Angeles respondents suggest that 46 percent are involuntary push-outs (expelled) or throwaways (allowed by parents to break away).

The large number of push-outs and throwaways reported has implications for the kinds of services that are needed. Either serious, highly intensive, family-oriented intervention is required or provisions need to be made for young people to conduct their lives outside of the family situation.

These data need to be seen against the considerable variation among individual agencies in the percentage of push-outs and throwaways they reported. The responses ranged from 5 percent to 95 percent. Thus, different agencies must take different programmatic approaches, depending on whether their clients are voluntarily or involuntarily homeless.

Reasons for Running Behavior

Communication and family disruption were the major reported reasons for running away. The figures suggest the need for services offering family therapy and conflict resolution, as well as attention to merged families and

the resulting tensions. **Improving communication among parents, steppar-
ents, and youth would be beneficial. Parental abuse—physical and sexual—
is also an important issue that has not received the attention it requires. The
scale of the problem seems larger than acknowledged, even by those who
recognize its existence.**

Reason Given by Youth for Running	*Percentage*
Communication difficulties with parents	73
Family disruption (divorce or separation)	55
Physical abuse	39
Sexual abuse	26
Wants to be on his or her own by choice	18

Almost three-quarters of the young people said they ran away because of
communication problems with parents. According to impressions of our respondents, this is consistent with general research findings (see Action Guideline IV,
Chapter 2). Family disruption, including divorce and separation, was the second
most common explanation offered by runaway and homeless youth for leaving
home (over 50 percent).

These two reasons were linked together by several experts. They observed
that, when pressures increase within the marital relationship, communication
with the children becomes secondary and more strained. One respondent
commented: "Some of these parents are trying so hard to maintain a stable
relationship of their own" that the needs of the children are neglected.

Respondents reported that a significant number of youth say they ran
because of abuse in the home: more than one-third ran away because of physical
abuse, and about one-fourth, because of sexual abuse. A majority of participants
remarked that often youth run because of abuse but "the true nature of the abuse"
does not emerge until they feel that they can trust the agency representative.
Thus, in some cases, youths leave the agency before revealing abuse as the
cause, perhaps contributing to a low estimate. In our survey interviews with
runaways, abuse was clearly a major reason for running away.

The connection between poor communications, family disruption, and
physical and sexual abuse were noted by many survey participants. The
single-parent and merged family are characterized by the introduction of an
unfamiliar adult, most often a stepfather "who tries to take over." Interviewees
reported that females were often abused by the stepfather or the mother's
boyfriend. Family disruption and physical abuse were also related to alcoholism
and drug use.

Respondents also reported that approximately 10 percent of their clients say
they ran because they wanted to be on their own. Many agency personnel believe
that only a small number of youth leave home for this reason. "They leave of
their own volition" because the family situation is intolerable and they are

seeking an escape. Thus, the actual percentage of youth who really want to be on their own may be smaller than the figures suggest.

Respondents gave many more reasons youth say they leave home, in addition to the categories listed in the questionnaire. Some runaways leave because of an unwanted pregnancy, school problems, or a "multiple placement history." The following reasons were offered by one interviewee: "Peer pressure, lack of parenting, and attention getting." One respondent noted: "There is *never* one single cause" for young people to run away from home. Many of the respondents indicated that the perception of being "unwanted" and "not belonging to a family" is a characteristic of runaways.

In general, the agencies offered no evidence to corroborate the runaways' complaints but rather "took the kids at their own word." In the case of claims of sexual and/or physical abuse, agency personnel contacted police and/or the Department of Public Social Services (DPSS).

Physical and Mental Health of Status Offenders

The physical and mental health of runaway and homeless youth is poor.

Overall, the informants characterized the physical health status of runaways as "poor," "lower than average," and "low energy." Among the list of reported ailments were sexually transmitted diseases (7), alcohol and drug abuse (5), malnourishment (3), and infections (including gynecological ones) (3). Poor hygiene, lice, and scabies were also noted (3). Three respondents mentioned the general lack of preventive health care, especially dental care. Other individual respondents noted dermatological disorders (particularly among hard-core runaways), family planning problems and ectopic pregnancies, broken bones, cuts and bruises, colds, tension headaches, eating disorders (bulimia and anorexia), hepatitis, and AIDS and pre-AIDS. A number of respondents said that physical health "depends on the kid's length of time on the streets." Since no checklist was provided in the questionnaire, these figures probably understate the extent of health problems. Only a few agencies focus on such problems in their work.

A large proportion of status offenders are "in trouble emotionally," "alienated," "distressed," and "disoriented." The most common characteristic of their mental health status observed by respondents was self-destructive and suicidal behavior. Agencies attributed these suicidal tendencies to the fact that these youth come from dysfunctional families and are prone to depression. The youth were described as having psychological problems, such as distorted and poor self-esteem, and psychotic, sociopathic, and behavioral disorders. This generally poor mental health, stemming from a negative home environment, contributed to the offenders' "inability to trust, inability to be intimate, and their capacity to abuse others." Half the clients are estimated to be into drug abuse and one-half, in alcohol abuse. Other stress-related problems were also identified, including legal difficulties, vocational counseling needs, lack of services for gays and lesbians, and language difficulties exacerbated by lack of Spanish-speaking agency workers.

Problem	Mean Percentage of Clients Cited by Respondents
Drug abuse	52
Alcohol abuse	51
Psychiatric	42
Physical health	25
Pregnancy[a]	9

[a]The percentage for pregnancy is inflated by a high proportion reported by a few agencies.

Typical Career of the Runaway and Agency Effect on Its Trajectory

About two-thirds of the agency respondents were of the opinion that they had at least some positive impact on the career trajectory of status offenders. Their contribution was mainly as role models of more positive people in more positive relationships. Many regarded as their aim the teaching of coping and survival skills. The one-third of respondents who felt their agencies had minimal or no effect on the runaway population blamed their ineffectiveness on a lack of time and resources. Some contended that changes in the "laws with no teeth," as well as increases in funding, would focus more attention on the status offender population.

Respondents from a wide variety of organizations (law enforcement, shelters, probation) asserted that the vast majority of status offenders came from highly negative or destructive environments. The unstable family situation consisted of a single parent, or a foster home or adoption home characterized by a "lack of nurturing." Ten respondents specifically mentioned either drug or alcohol abuse and family violence—physical, emotional, and sexual (including incest)—as situations from which youth decide to run. Parents often cannot cope with the child who is fighting back, and the child rebels by fleeing or is pushed out. One respondent observed that runaways come from extreme environments—either too lax (home and foster home) or too restrictive (home or juvenile hall).

Where adolescents run depends upon the program visibility. One-quarter of the knowledgeable individuals stated that initially they may live in abandoned cars, hotels, or buildings, or become a "house mouse." A "savior" finds a young person on the street and becomes a sexual partner in exchange for providing food, clothing, and shelter. When the older person "gets tired of babysitting and kicks the kid out," the youth goes back to the streets or to a police station rather than returning home. If they go back to the streets, they usually get involved in hustling, drug dealing, or petty crime. Two respondents noted that the police station is not a promising alternative because of the lack of adequate placement options for teens. Police may try to take an unwilling youngster back home. Marginal youth with a past record might end up in a juvenile hall.

One respondent summed up the outlook for these children: "The long-term prospects for this population are poor," both emotionally and financially. Future job prospects are poor because of the types of current problems (alcohol, drug abuse) from which they suffer. Fifty percent of the respondents observed that status offenders lacked education, leading to bleak or marginal employment prospects: "They can make more money turning a trick or selling drugs than they can in a minimum wage job at a fast food restaurant." This population does not "excel later in life because of the large void in their education and lack of healthy peer relationships." One respondent observed that some consider going into the military to get an education and better paying jobs.

A shaky prognosis for the emotional future of status offenders is implied by repetition of this pattern. One-fourth of the respondents observed that a portion of this population "drifts from odd jobs and casual relationships which produce offspring that follow the same pattern." They "engage in physically and emotionally battering relationships" that provide the model for their own children. Two respondents suggested that the pattern repeats itself because there is no service continuity: "We serve a patchwork function, filling the holes (food, clothing, shelter) to make traveling easier."

Only a minority of experts believe that some status offenders grow out of their problems. Those who don't like school stop "illegal" acts of truancy when they reach the age of eighteen. Some children who are "acting out" stop being "rotten kids" when they have a job with financial rewards and adult responsibilities.

CURRENT PROGRAMS AND SERVICES

State of Status Offender Services

Knowledgeable individuals viewed community services for runaways negatively. This is because of a lack of systematic planning, financial and human resources, and legal constraints. [There have been improvements in these areas since the survey.]

The experts were asked to give their views at the most general level about the current state of status offender services in Los Angeles County. The responses were not encouraging:

Nothing is being done	14
Very little or not enough is being done	10
Other	4

The majority of the respondents to this question said little or nothing is being done to serve juvenile runaways adequately and half declared "nothing." Nearly a third (eight) of those interviewed believed that status offenders are "falling through the cracks," victims of "a lack of systematic, planned services for them." The respondents are concerned that there should be sufficient personnel and other resources to intervene early, that interested agencies should not work at cross-purposes, and that the county should "not act residually and in a piecemeal fashion."

Those criticizing the lack or limited availability of services make a distinction between the public and private sectors. For a few respondents, the private agencies provide most of the services, particularly short-term shelter and therapeutic care. Others complain about the limited services provided by the public sector, especially a decline in Probation Department and other county resources for the status offender.

Four experts attribute the poor state of current Los Angeles County status offender services to an absence of legal constraints. Current "law is too lax and doesn't give social agencies the authority or a handle to work effectively with the kids"; it "has no teeth." Thus, "the agencies have no legal clout with the kids any more . . . especially those who need the authority and structure represented by detention."

Availability and Adequacy of Programs and Services

Agencies usually offered several different services, with a mean of 4.8 and a range from 1 to 10. In ratings of quality, there was little agreement: only three services were named by more than 20 percent of the respondents from agencies; four were given high ratings but only by four or five respondents each.

The variations in service and the number of agencies reporting are indicated below. Because replies were in response to an open-ended question rather than to a checklist, some of these services may have been taken for granted or overlooked, thus appearing to be underrepresented.

Counseling	
Individual (short- and long-term)	13
Group counseling	6
Family counseling	5
Crisis intervention	3
Hotline	2
Referrals	
To shelters and social services	10
Shelter	9
Medical services	5

Legal and advocacy services	5
Job development and vocational training	4
Food	4
Clothing	4
Tutoring and special education	3
Miscellaneous	
Cultural activities	1
Sports and recreation	1
Basic survival skills	1

Some counseling opportunities were offered by almost all of the agencies offering services directly to runaways. Close to 50 percent of the agencies offering individual counseling also offered family and/or group counseling. Often this treatment took the form of an initial hot-line call or crisis intervention measure prior to a shelter or other social service referral. Slightly more than half of the respondents included referrals as a service they provided.

Another way of looking at problems is to examine the problems youth bring to agencies. The Hollywood Homeless Youth Project (1985) kept an accurate record of all requests received and produced the following listing.

Hollywood Homeless Youth Project

	Clients	
Services Initially Requested	*Number*	*Percentage*
Job training and placement	174	86
Shelter	102	50
School	98	48
Need identification	73	36
Food	64	32
Clothing	54	27
Medical care	44	22
Individual counseling	38	19
Family counseling	10	5
Legal help	11	5
Protection from danger	6	3
Drug or alcohol problem	6	3
Questions about sex	7	3

Actual services provided included shelter; job assistance; individual, family, task-oriented, and psychodynamic counseling; foster family placement; and independent living assistance.

Along with shelter, individual counseling, food (and often clothing), medical care, and legal and advocacy assistance (assistance in obtaining identification, birth certificates, welfare, social security numbers, and in interfacing with other agencies) were also provided.

Medical and advocacy assistance was cited by five agencies. The medical treatment was delivered in a clinic while emergency care was provided by a hospital associated with the agency.

Job development and vocational training were program components of four agencies. Two of these agencies offered tutoring and special education assistance as well. Basic survival skills (check writing, apartment hunting, etc.), cultural activities, and sports and recreation services were each cited by one respondent.

Concerning their views about adequacy of services, respondents cited many different services as doing a good job, sometimes noting specific agencies and sometimes noting categories of service providers. Only three services were named by more than 20 percent of the interviewees. Shelters were generally rated as less than fair, and the counseling agencies were seen as doing only a fair job. Programs and services available to status offenders were perceived overall as either overburdened or limited by resource deficits and legal restrictions.

These findings both agree with and differ from those of a national survey of runaway and homeless youth agencies. The 210 agencies surveyed in that instance judged that they "work well" and that they have "dealt effectively with an increasing 'at-risk' population of youth" (National Network of Runaway and Youth Services, 1985: 22). The ratings were made strictly by the service-providing agencies themselves and were not balanced by the views of other informed and interested observers in the community, as they were in the Los Angeles County survey. However, the conclusion that local agencies are overburdened and resource-poor is mirrored by the national study.

Homogeneous or Diverse Agency Clientele

Government agencies, such as law enforcement, probation, the courts, and other public social services, tend to deal with multiple status offender categories and refer cases to one another. In addition, public agencies make some referrals, although perhaps in a limited way, to smaller voluntary organizations, which tend to offer more specialized programs for subpopulations of status offenders—truants, hard-core runaways, long-distance runaways, and so on. These voluntary agencies seem to make referrals more often to one another than to governmental departments. The governmental and voluntary agencies appear to constitute separate service systems functioning alongside one another, with only limited interaction.

Agencies indicated service categories as follows:

Serve specialized population	16
Runaway	10
Homeless	2
Truants	4
Serve mixed population	11

The largest group of agencies in the survey dealt with specialized subgroups. The subpopulations identified by offense were predominantly runaway and homeless youth and truants. Agencies with a focus on runaway and homeless youth further differentiated the targeted populations by sex, length of time away from home, distance from home, and in other ways.

Three agencies worked exclusively with females. Seven of the agencies designed programs aimed at youth who were first-time runaways. Two agencies sought to serve the needs of the "chronic, hard-core, streetwise" homeless youth. In addition to counseling services, each of these two agencies provided a different focused service, such as medical care or vocational counseling. Two agencies served long-distance runaways and made themselves visible in the downtown area through outreach staff and flyers. These two agencies targeted runaways who congregate at the transportation (bus and train) depots. One agency serving long-distance runaways reported that a large portion of its clients were youth "leaving Central America with their families' blessings."

Two agencies that served multiple status offender categories specialized in other ways: one group focused on the parents of status offenders (Toughlove) and the other, on self-identified gays and lesbians.

A total of four of the agencies served truants. Two of these organizations were sponsored by the school system, and two were based outside of the schools. Three of this set of agencies dealt exclusively with truants, while one served truants and a small number of incorrigibles.

Repeat Service to Clients by Agencies

All agencies reported some repeat activity, most commonly in the 5–10 percent range, and most found they were dealing with some clients who had been seen by other agencies.

On the average, 19 percent of the clients reported to be seen by county agencies were repeaters. This figure is raised, however, by the high percentages reported by law enforcement agencies and by two private agencies who do a great deal of outreach on the street level and have a high level of contact with youth. Many of the youth apparently reappear in the Los Angeles area after having been returned home.

Some runaway and homeless youth apparently approach several agencies. Agencies said that most of their clientele have had previous involvement with other agencies. On the average, about two-thirds of the agencies have seen youth who were seen by another agency beforehand. Ten of the eighteen agencies responding to this question indicated previous involvement, and the percentages are uniformly high.

Seasonal Variations in Service Provision

The major holidays are a low point in client demand. These periods allow staff time to vacation and rest, do forward planning, catch up, or work intensively with selected clients. Shelters and referral centers may need supplementary staff during the summer months.

The responses of individuals to the inquiry were as follows:

Steady flow	8
Seasonal variations	23
Decrease during holiday periods	13
Increase during summer months	7
Decrease during summer months	3

Respondents agreed that most of the youth go home for the holidays, especially between Thanksgiving and Christmas. Law enforcement agencies and school officials noted a decrease in the number of status offenders served in the summer months, attributable to a reduction in truancy cases because of the school vacation. The increase for the referral network agencies and shelters begins in the late spring, peaks in the summer, and tapers off when school begins in the fall.

KEY ISSUES

The Los Angeles County survey asked about several key issues that provoke controversy or uncertainty in the field. It was hoped that the study might indicate where there are points of consensus in these contentious areas.

Lessons and Experience Before and After
Deinstitutionalization of Status Offenders

There is strong disagreement over the need for secure detention as a way of providing therapeutic and other services, although respondents overwhelmingly agree on the need for special treatment approaches for the juvenile

runaway clients. Consequently, counter to the deinstitutionalization philosophy, half of the local experts favor some form of secure detention as an available option, in order to begin the treatment process. The experts add two limitations. First, detention would be a short-term experience, so that youth would not become lost in secure detention. Second, detention would be used with a limited sector of the status offender population, the small percentage of youth who are out of control. But one-third of the interviewees strongly opposed secure detention and viewed status offenders as victims in need of therapeutic and other community-based services. For these respondents, it is futile to lock up status offenders.

The question of secure detention for status offenders is perhaps the most explosive in the field and probably the most troubling consequence of the 1974 federal Juvenile Justice and Delinquency Prevention legislation and the 1977 Dixon bill in California (which prohibits secure detention of juvenile status offenders). The answers by individuals to the survey questions showed this distribution:

We need some form of secure detention	14
We don't need secure detention	9
Uncertain or inapplicable	2
No response regarding detention	3

The responses indicated both a split and uncertainty on the subject of secure detention. For half (fourteen) of the respondents to this question, the lesson learned is that some form of secure detention for the juvenile status offender is useful. The position of this diverse group, which includes representatives of the school system, law enforcement, the juvenile justice system, and service providers from both the public and private sectors, is exemplified by the comments of one respondent, who believed that "limited detention enabled us to start a treatment process, showing status offenders that someone really cared. Nowadays they can just split and we lose a chance at diagnosis and early treatment." At the same time, this respondent realized that youth become lost in secure detention, so it is not being advocated as *the* means of solving the problem. Detention is seen as "a short-term, limited approach serving as a basis from which to refer to helpful programs." Others echoed this remark: "The term 'lock-up' is misunderstood; we just want to get the kids some help"; "Secure detention of some . . . 601s should be made an available option"; "Short-term detention is occasionally necessary but not available"; and "Some kids need secure detention so they can be helped."

Six respondents decried the adverse consequences of deinstitutionalization for the juvenile justice system and for legal authority-based efforts to aid the status offender. Mostly justice system and school personnel, these respondents believe that "juvenile court authority [pre-Dixon] was helpful"; that "pre-Dixon we could do a lot more. . . . You could have things hanging over a kid's head";

and "therapeutic detention was possible." Since these laws were passed, experts believe that juvenile court judges lack the necessary legislative backing to deal with the status offender population. According to them, "the teeth have been taken out of . . . programs." A school respondent said: "After Dixon's bill, other agencies—Probation Department, Juvenile Court—have been constrained. Now they're hardly involved, as they lack the ability to follow up and follow through. They can't compete." Detention is particularly needed to affect "the 1 percent or 2 percent who are out of control . . . ; this would then have a spillover or Hawthorne effect, favorably influencing the behavior of other youth."

Almost all of these detention advocates (twelve of fourteen) stressed the necessity of special treatment resources for the status offender. In fact, for eight of these respondents, the lesson learned is that "status offenders and criminal offenders should not be treated as one population." One expert said: "The problem was that they were held in Juvenile Hall in a youth detention facility and they came out smarter about criminal activity and more streetwise." They should be held "in a separate special place for up to one month so that they can be evaluated." The concept of a special place for status offenders is noted, as well, in the responses of other interviewees who want secure detention to resemble a "boarding school with a fence, something not as depressing as juvenile hall," something "homelike . . . not punishment." Under such involuntary residential conditions, runaways would receive needed counseling and reconciliation services. As a couple of respondents also noted, parents would also then receive the support needed to handle their children's problems. It was pointed out that the same effects can be achieved not through lock-up but by saturation staffing. Putting enough staff into high-intensity situations with youth can have powerful restraining effects.

The large and diverse group of interviewees, however, did not agree with respect to detention. Nearly one-third of those who responded (nine of twenty-eight) agreed that "what we learned pre-Dixon was that lock-up won't work." They agreed with the expert who said: "We do not need secure detention at all. We need to try a therapeutic approach with individuals, families, and groups." Their position is that the status offender does not belong in the criminal justice system, for "we know now that many are victims." We need the resources for specialized programs and a plan to aid status offenders, especially in situations such as the dysfunctional family, "alcoholism on the part of parents, divorce, separation and remarriage." Those who oppose secure detention believe that "it will be abused," and, consequently, we should "try to get along without it." Abuse means overuse. Once detention is allowed, it will become a crutch to be used with many youth, including those to whom it does not apply at all. For these respondents, detention is like opening Pandora's box.

Two respondents added: "We've never given deinstitutionalization a real chance because legislation never provided funding for community-based alternatives." Another service provider pointedly inquired: "If we do have the ability to hold kids, do we have the appropriate rehabilitative services to offer them?"

Communication and Coordination Among Agencies

The respondents came down squarely in favor of more coordination and cited grave problems of poor interaction between both the public and the private sector agencies, and within each sector, which inhibit effective service provision. To improve the current level of communication and coordination, many respondents suggested a leading role for an appropriately staffed Department of Children's Services (DCS). [Since this survey, a coordinating body has been established through state funds and DCS has created a special runaway service program.]

The Los Angeles situation is uniquely influenced by a recently created Department of Children's Services, which is a totally independent county department reporting directly to the Board of Supervisors. DCS has been given the mission of vigorously tending to the needs of children and youth, including runaways. Some community activists view it as a powerful advocate for teenage runaways; others question its commitment to the adolescent population.

There has been, on the one hand, a strong tradition of support in American social welfare for voluntary action as well as for organizational freedom and autonomy among agencies. On the other hand, the social welfare system has been criticized as being peculiarly fragmented, competitive, and inefficient.

One questionnaire item asked respondents to estimate the degree of coordination and communication among Los Angeles agencies. The amount of coordination was assessed by individual respondents as follows:

A lot	0
Some/Limited	14
Very little/Hardly any	13
Don't know	1

The experts agreed in their view that there has been absence of active communication and coordination among service-providing agencies. About one-half (thirteen) of the respondents saw hardly any communication and coordination, while the others (fourteen) note a limited degree of agency and program interaction. For some in the former group, there is "poor coordination and information sharing," where "there are turf problems and a competition for funds." One respondent believed that youth lose because agencies vie for the same funds to develop similar programs. Probation, DCS, and mental health agencies are perceived as not talking to one another. While "most programs and agencies are probably aware of each other . . . there's a lot of misunderstanding of what each really does," with "each agency . . . critical of the others" as well. Consequently, the overall assessment that "there's no real working together" is not surprising.

Others are concerned with the absence of an official level "meeting of the key people involved with status offenders." They see a "need . . . for a regular forum among all types of agencies, public and private, providing services, for each has a piece of knowledge that they can't put together at present." "We need a coordinating agency, . . . but one that acknowledges local community interests and problems" and is based on a structure of "regional committees or councils with representatives from the various agencies concerned."

Those respondents (fourteen) who thought there was some communication and coordination focused on the limited developments within the private, not-for-profit sector where "they network for survival." They mentioned the "generally O.K." communication between agencies engaged primarily in counseling and offering private runaway shelters. An example is the impact of a shared funding source, cited by a couple of the respondents, as a vehicle for promoting communication and coordination: "Having a single or common funding source forces agencies to come together," and "United Way has this effect on agencies as well." But the genuineness of this communication and collaboration was questioned by one respondent: "Many of these efforts are strictly for publicity and funding purposes. The Privacy Act actually compromised true collaborative efforts, with less emphasis today on sharing information regarding a particular child or family."

Nearly one-third (eight) of the respondents pointed to the gap between the public and private sectors, "between the traditional agencies [County] and the nonprofit agencies." As one respondent said, efforts at communication and coordination "are constrained by the problem of volume and the restriction this places on the ability to follow up on individual cases." How receptive to coordination can we expect personnel to be if they are already feeling overburdened?

One law enforcement representative thought that the "police have been picking up the pieces" left by unsuccessful communication. A shelter agency respondent acknowledged this problem indirectly by praising the Hollywood Police Division for its "seminars with different agencies." A couple of other interviewees, however, criticized police actions toward status offenders and toward the agencies serving runaways. One agency person said: "Communication with police is not very good because the police have a poor perception of community resources; they see agencies as a refuge from the law." The respondent believed the high crime rate among the street population served contributes to the police perception. Another provider complained that "police roust [harass] kids."

Planning on a Generalized or Targeted Basis

There is clear support for services addressing the specific needs of different status offender subpopulations.

Some professionals thought all clients should be treated as equal in order to ensure fairness and consistency in services and treatment. For others, clients break down into distinct subpopulations requiring separate and even unequal treatment. Obviously, the issue has important implications for the planning of services. The replies to the survey question were as follows:

Status Offender Population

Subpopulations	17
One population	8
Uncertain	3

The majority of respondents who replied here defined the need to approach problems in the context of particular subpopulations. Runaways need differentiated services, depending on whether they are chronic "street kids" or youth temporarily experiencing a family crisis. A variety of special subpopulations of status offenders were listed by the interviewees, including younger and older; gay and lesbian; sexually abused (incest victims or prostitutes); and those with particular sociocultural factors associated with ethnic and family background. One expert said: "We can't assume that ethnic families will respond to the same approach used with the white middle-class ones," especially where "families are culturally encouraged not to air the family's dirty laundry."

Prospects for Returning Home

Only a portion of the runaway population have good prospects for family reunification. For others, alternative arrangements must be made. The survey data suggest that four distinct service modalities are necessary to provide for four different away-from-home populations:

1. **Family intervention services to facilitate reconciliation and reunion with the natural family (about one-half of the clients);**
2. **Substitute facilities, such as a group home or foster care (close to one-third);**
3. **Preparation for independent living, including help in locating and setting up an apartment, in acquiring skills to obtain a job, and in becoming connected with a suitable helping network (about 5 percent); and**
4. **Different service offerings, whose character is not altogether clear, but including medical assistance and food for established street dwellers (20 percent).**

It is important to know how far it is feasible to aim toward reuniting children with their families. If a return to the family is not possible, then alternative services and facilities have to be arranged. When experts were asked what percentage of current clients have different disposition prospects, their opinions fell into the following categories:

Category	*Percentage*
Return home	47
Substitute facilities	29
Independent living	7
Street life	20

A little less than 50 percent of youthful clients are viewed as having a realistic prospect of returning to their homes, although there is considerable variation from agency to agency. Police organizations have the highest level of expectation of return to the home.

There is disagreement even among those reporting reasonable percentages about prospects for returning home. One found that "50 percent do go home [but that is] because there is no other choice and they acclimate somehow"; the other said that the percentage able to return home has declined from a high of 80 percent, as "the number of homeless kids is increasing." Of four respondents reporting a minority returning home, one said that the "home situations of our kids are often so bad that we don't want them to go back." A referral agency respondent bluntly stated that, of the youth they deal with, "practically none have a realistic prospect of returning home." (The young people surveyed in the Los Angeles County study strongly agreed.) About 30 percent of the clients "have a realistic prospect for successful substitute or out-of-home placement." Again, there is variation by agency.

Only a small minority of clients now being served by respondent agencies or programs were viewed as "ready for emancipation." A very high proportion of the interviewees (fifteen of eighteen) think the proportion is 10 percent or less of the youth currently being seen. However, apparently three respondents assume a support system for such youth: those "ready for emancipation" are defined as youth "eligible for general relief."

Some 20 percent of youthful clientele were described as "sophisticated, streetwise kids . . . currently living on their own," but only one program—the High Risk Youth Project at Children's Hospital—described a majority of its clientele thus. One respondent stressed: "These kids don't need counseling; rather they need practical information about looking after themselves." Without it, as another interviewee noted, "living on their own . . . translates into taking up residence in cars, doorways, on roofs, in parks, shelters and . . . other temporary arrangements."

Overreliance on family therapy in a global fashion can be dysfunctional and confining. At the same time, a substantial proportion of the clients can benefit from this approach.

POLICY AND PROGRAM RECOMMENDATIONS

In the final phase of the survey, the knowledgeable individuals were asked to make specific recommendations for policies and programs to address problems of status offenders, particularly runaway and homeless youth. Although there are action implications in most of the questions asked in the first two sections, here the policy question was put directly. Respondents were asked what they believe a central public child service agency (such as DCS) should do, what other local organizations should undertake, what action should be initiated by the state, and what the federal government should contribute. The experts were asked what program strategies should be top priority for the central child agency and what geographic areas of the county are underserved and should be bolstered. The survey probed the kind of preventive strategies that ought to be mounted. It also sought views of the main obstacles to carrying out these actions.

Actions of a Central Public Child Service Agency at the Local Level

The research staff anticipated that the responses would focus on specific programs and techniques, such as vocational training, long-term shelter, transitional services, or on particular subpopulations, such as older, streetwise youth, Hispanics, or those from out of the county. Unexpectedly, the overwhelming emphasis was on system level functional issues: making the pattern of service delivery within the county more unified, comprehensive, and effective.

Listed below are all program recommendations that received six or more mentions. According to the respondents, a central child service agency should:

1. Establish a rational, integrated, and systematic approach to serving young people (sixteen);
2. Arrange for better cooperation, communication, and coordination among service providers (nine);
3. Increase staff competency through staff training and development programs (nine);
4. Give greater priority and commitment to this problem (six); and
5. Provide more contracts to voluntary agencies for service delivery (six).

Systematic Planning and Coordination. A majority of the respondents focused on system planning issues. They wanted a more rational, cohesive service delivery network, as they said in comments like these:

- "The agency should broaden its sights and look at the whole problem— overall planning is the most important thing."

- "The agency should conduct a needs assessment to find out what has to be done. There should be a comprehensive institutional response."
- "The agency should establish guidelines for defining the different types of status offenders and what kinds of services are needed by each type."
- "The agency should be a central information and referral agent. This means making maximum use of all existing community resources and channeling kids into the right place to obtain the services they need."

Respondents felt a child welfare service agency should assume leadership in helping to shape and manage an orderly, integrated system of service delivery, and none, including the voluntary sector, expressed resentment about the agency's taking steps to do so.

Cooperation and Communication. The same sentiment was expressed about the agency's role in fostering interagency cooperation and communications for the purpose of sharing information and reducing some of the competition identified already as a major block to problem solving. Comments included:

- "The agency should help with communication and integration among services."
- "The agency should be a liaison with private agencies."
- "It should create a foster care network."
- "The agency should be a clearinghouse for services and should encourage countywide communication and coordination."

Staff Development. Staff training and development also received priority attention among the survey participants. Many thought that some personnel lacked the general expertise, skills, and attitudes needed for working with the clients. Some comments describing the general problem were:

- "There is a lack of expertise on these matters."
- "The agency needs to improve the quality, expertise, and effectiveness of staff working in this area."

Some specific technical and performance areas needing attention were identified:

- "The agency needs to train its workers to deal in a consistent way with their own regulations. Shelters have contact with many different workers and they all interpret the regulations differently."
- "Staff people have to learn to use authority in a different way in working with adolescents."

Some remarked on attitudes:

- "Probation officers and social workers think these kids are brats and nymphomaniacs, just doing whatever they want and not working at any job."
- "You have to change the awareness of the staff. Kids with punk haircuts and big mouths can still be victims."

Agency Commitment to the Problem. While there was support for the child service agency's key role, respondents were cautious about the agency's willingness to muster the energy and resources needed to carry it out. The agency was urged to mobilize itself to tackle several problems:

- "The agency needs to recognize its obligation to adolescent minors."
- "The agency needs to make this population a priority, with no fudging. The adolescent cases need to be brought near the top of the in-box, not buried at the bottom of the pile."
- "There has to be awareness of the worth of these matters." (As a consequence of this study the agency has initiated a service geared to adolescent runaways.)

Contracts with Agencies. A number of respondents emphasized that the central public child service agency should provide contracts to voluntary agencies in straight declaratory terms. It is clear that agency representatives see a central public agency as a source of funds to support their programs. It is also implied that voluntary agencies possess certain characteristics—intimacy, flexibility, small scale, and caring staff attitudes—that should be valued and that a large bureaucratic entity cannot replicate.

Contracts are also related to greater dependability and regularity on the part of the central agency in following through. As one respondent put it, "Public agencies must act in good faith with the voluntary ones. Voluntary agencies have gotten strung out so often by having their funds withdrawn suddenly that they are very cautious about setting up new contract arrangements."

A Youth View. The runaway youth interviewed want *long-term facilities* in which they can remain *voluntarily* and receive appropriate *counseling*. These recommendations were based on the collective experiences of youth who explicitly described the dangers (drug dealers, pimps) and explained the trap into which so many runaways fall because services are neither available nor sufficiently visible. "In general, more money and more attention by the county would help runaways," they said.

They said that social agencies help them to "get life situated." Assistance took the form of reconciliation services, placement with a family or a shelter, school registration, and counseling. One girl observed that the agency helped her to stop running away as her means of avoiding conflicts at home.

The youth expressed disappointment in dealing with social service agencies that "believed parents and adults rather than the runaway." The youth reported being "pushed back" to their homes. Returning home "did more harm than good" if the home situation had not been thoroughly assessed by the agency. This evaluation was especially important for foster homes and adoptions, particularly follow-up interviews with the families and "surprise" visits by the agency. Unannounced dropping in did not allow the adults to "fix things up and lie." In addition, the youth responded that there were "not enough services for older kids—everyone wants five-year-olds."

The young people interviewed asked for long-term facilities, places "to stay where a kid cannot be held," operating on a voluntary basis, in contrast to the restrictiveness of juvenile hall. An alternative placement facility should have "beds, telephones, freedom, a relaxed atmosphere and nice people," they said.

The young clients interviewed explained the need for counseling services integrated into long-term facilities and available to youth who have been reconciled with their families. The youth saw ongoing treatment as essential to their emotional progress. They recommended that counseling be offered at varying levels of intensity. Some youth require intensive counseling, while others merely need referrals for food or shelter. Based upon their experiences, they observed "different levels of urgency" and "different levels of coping" skills among their runaway peers.

Voluntary Agency Recommendations

Like the recommendations for the public child welfare service agency, the main response concerning voluntary agencies was that community agencies should improve their cooperation, communication, and coordination.

Community organizations were asked to make a greater commitment to the runaway problem and to the age group. Funding was primary, with equal focus on voluntary community agencies raising more money to deal with the problem and receiving more funds to do so through contracts. The main replies included:

- Cooperation, communication, coordination
- Greater commitment to the problem
- Raising funds
- Receiving contracts

These are typical of comments made on cooperation, communication, and coordination:

- "We need to try to work together to overcome turf and communication problems."
- "We end up being competitive about funding and the kids end up being victims again."
- "It's necessary to look at all the available resources and have a cooperative approach by all the agencies."

Greater commitment means expending more time, money, and effort:

- "Agencies need to recognize what they are dealing with and to invest the time, money, and effort required to solve the problem."
- "Agencies have to expand the services they are offering."

One observation about increased fundraising suggested alternative sources:

- "Corporations will often give money for these kinds of causes if approached in the right way. We should make greater use of private resources, like insurance, to support programs. Many parents don't realize that their insurance will cover some of the services that their kids need."

The once-mentioned items give an intriguing melange of the range of views about voluntary agencies. According to the respondents, agencies should:

- Become more visible about the services they offer;
- Work more cooperatively with law enforcement;
- Be able to call on the police for backup;
- Work with grass-roots groups for support and enthusiasm;
- Use stricter management procedures;
- Provide service to hard-to-place youth when all else fails;
- Improve working relationship between the school system and agencies;
- Provide more residential programs;
- Recognize the high level of disturbance among some youth;
- Develop transitional living facilities for hard-core youth;
- Emphasize family approaches;
- Provide more long-term treatment; and
- Support schools in dealing with truancy problems.

State Actions

The state should provide more funding, according to a majority of the respondents.

Seventeen respondents said financing should be the state's main contribution. Four others supported pending programmatic bills, which also had financial implications.

Another suggestion receiving substantial support was the provision of short-term detention for status offenders. Two people asked that (1) the state delineate legal responsibility and jurisdiction for status offenders and that (2) the state participate in coordinating services. A variety of individual responses included:

- Help homeless youth;
- Give police more support;
- Clarify service eligibility;
- Provide for training of law enforcement officers;
- Provide more psychiatric facilities;
- Define the status offender populations and differential services;
- Provide for serving severely emotionally disturbed youth; and
- Provide for hard-core streetwise runaways.

Federal Actions

Like that of the state, the main role of the federal government would be to provide more funding.

Apparently, respondents felt that the problem of status offenders and runaways is primarily a local one, and the professional resources to deal with it should be available at that level. Federal funds need to be channeled to the local level.

Long-Term Prevention of Runaway Behavior

The community experts agreed on several strategies for long-term prevention of runaway problems: reliance on schools, parenting education, early in-school intervention, and the use of natural helping networks.

Schools. The school is the only institution that has intimate contact with all children. It provides for interaction with parents and offers the most accessible setting in which to identify children with problems. Since teachers are often the only adult nonfamily members who have continuing contact with children, they can play an important role, not only in imparting information about parenting, but also in identifying emerging difficulties before they erupt into a crisis.

Parenting Education. Parenting education should be developed for both children and their parents and should specifically acknowledge the special stresses on single-parent families, including (as one respondent put it) "attendant problems such as maintaining one's own existence and keeping a relationship alive."

Among the themes that such programs should address are self-esteem, coping skills, communication, and issues of parental control. "What we see is a strong indication of parents unable or unwilling to exercise effective control. . . . They discipline not enough or too much," said one expert. Another expert said: "Parenting education is a broad conception that encompasses self-esteem issues and the learning of decision-making, as well as dealing with developmental issues. . . . If parents' self-esteem is raised, this is passed on to their kids."

Early Intervention in Schools. The recommendation for early in-school intervention was based on a shared belief among respondents that problems begin early and do not just suddenly emerge at age twelve or thirteen. One member of the panel said: "We know very early on (by second grade) what characteristics are going to lead to severe problems down the road, yet the situation is still malleable. We should put our resources there (K-3) for parent counseling, special education, etc."

Another expert emphasized the significance of the sixth grade to the junior high transition period, which coincides with critical periods for physical and emotional development. He suggested concentrating counseling and other resources at that important juncture (grades 5–7) to prepare both students and parents for the attendant stresses and to provide ongoing support as they work through them. Still other respondents noted that teaching decision-making skills, beginning in the early grades, could have a significant preventive impact. One direct outcome could be prevention of sexual abuse. Peer dynamics could also be harnessed productively in these early grades. "Kids are the chief resource for one another," observed one of the experts.

Natural Helping Networks. Another prevention strategy mentioned by a significant proportion of the respondents was the enhancement of what might be called local "mediating structures," natural helping systems, such as churches and neighborhood organizations. After-school programs or drop-in centers would give youth an opportunity to talk with others. Parenting groups sponsored by the YMCA, YWCA, or local family service agencies could extend the same opportunity to parents.

In other words, a communitywide response to the stresses experienced by families is needed. As one respondent noted, "We need programs addressing conflicts between parent and child at an early stage, before laws have been broken."

Obstacles to Progress

The major obstacles identified were lack of commitment on the part of governmental agencies, manifested in inadequate funding and staffing, and poor coordination among agencies.

A useful way to probe into a problem is to ask about the forces impeding its solution. When this question was posed to the survey participants, they answered:

Societal indifference	26
Funds, staff, other resources	19
Societal awareness and public understanding	7
Coordination among agencies	14
Defining and differentiating the population	5
Lack of parental responsibility	3
Inadequate legislative statutes	2

A total of twenty-six respondents referred to the lack of community understanding and commitment as the key obstacle to effective action. Specific comments include:

- "Basically, we are dealing with adult attitudes. People don't want to put forth the resources because this is a group that is not attractive."
- "There is a lack of understanding on the part of the community and local politicians of the nature of the problem and its severity. Something is very wrong with the family."
- "Resources are not available and there is a lack of knowledge generally about what to do about the problem."
- "There is insufficient community awareness—we need more publicity. Parents must recognize their responsibility to such kids."

A faulty pattern of community networking again was blamed:

- "There is a lack of clarity of roles among actors in the system; jurisdictional problems involved who has responsibility for what kids."
- "There isn't enough honesty among agencies and no responsibility taking."
- "Communication is a big problem. DCS doesn't really know what shelters can do for kids and tends to see the shelters as places to store them. This leads to an adversarial relationship."

Another problem concerns the defining and sorting out of the youth population. In part this is a cognitive problem (identifying and diagnosing clients) and in part it is one of coordination among units of the system.

Parental lack of responsibility is also perceived as a factor that impedes solutions. The family is seen as crucial in both preventing and solving the problem. The legislation is not giving enough "teeth" to service providers through detention facilities and compliance provisions in truancy laws.

A variety of other obstacles were identified by a single respondent each: lack of awareness within the service system, deterioration of the family, insufficient day care support for working mothers, rigidity in procedures of social agencies, lack of imagination and ingenuity in agency response, lack of quality programs, the federal government's emphasis on rugged individualism, lack of understanding by law enforcement of what is possible within the current law, local government not taking enough responsibility, "the kids are not motivated—they don't want help."

The survey identified critical problems and recommended solutions regarding runaway and homeless youth. Chapter 5 focuses on avenues of potentially positive action, crystallizing fundamental policy options for runaway and homeless youth. The responses of community experts are integrated with the results of the synthesis of existing empirical research in formulating policy options.

GETTING ORGANIZED

(Administrators Talk About Their Agencies)

SAFE HOUSE

We've been funded to bring a new approach to the problem of homeless youth. At this point, we've completed our planning and will be starting operations within two weeks. I can tell you more about intentions than accomplishments.

The program that we're setting up is designed primarily as a demonstration project to get kids off the streets. That is our basic focus. Safe House will try to stabilize them with whatever that takes. We will place a lot of emphasis on our shelter, which will be combined with social support. Access into our system is through the shelter services that we're offering at the Longwood YMCA. It will be a day care center during the day, and when they fold up we come in and turn it into a homeless youth center at night. We have twenty-three beautiful futons in designer colors that arrived yesterday, which we will be stacking and laying out in the shelter. We're thinking of carrying out an all-Japanese theme: come in, take your shoes off, get thongs, and process through.

We will be running a group every night at the shelter. Some of these will be therapeutic groups. Some will be social groups. Part of what we see as our obligation is to help create a pure support system as effective as the pure support system on the streets. We know that an awful lot of the kids on the streets felt like outsiders in their own communities. When they first hit the streets, they found a culture they sensed they belonged to.

Now, we may look at the values of that culture and have some reservations about how productive, how healthy all of it is. But these kids are obviously getting some basic goodies. I think it's our obligation to understand those goodies and to be able to provide a healthier version. One of the things the kids experience as good is mutual support. They're finding compatible shared values.

What we're trying to do is set the same thing up but in a much safer situation and one that's going to lead toward stability. We are having groups every night. Hopefully, the kids will find that it is a way to connect with one another and find out that they are not alone in what they're going through. There is help available.

Our shelter will be opening 8 o'clock every evening, and from 8 to 11 o'clock we will be doing intake at the "Y" as long as space is available. During the day, intake will be through a counseling center down the street. At the "Y," we will be having curfew at 11 o'clock, and at 11:30 lights will go out. Aside from those kids who are up because they are in crisis talking to our staff, we are going to have some peaceful evenings.

The shelter closes at 8 o'clock in the morning with the provision of vouchers to each of the kids so that they can get a good breakfast at the Friendship Cafe, which is run by the "Y." So the kids will get dinner at night and breakfast in the morning. And that will be part of the package.

We're setting it up this loose way because we know that street kids are fearful of agencies and fearful of adults. We will make it as easy for them to come into the system as possible. One of our techniques is saying that for the first seventy-two hours we are requiring nothing except understanding the basic rules—no drugs or alcohol. No sex on the premises. No violence or threats of violence.

We are setting it up so that all these kids need to do is observe those rules and tell us a name that they would like to be called while they are working with us. We're not asking for any more, unless *they* are looking for something more immediate. What we are letting them do is spend the first 72 hours feeling out the environment, talking to the other kids, finding out if we're okay people to work with, and learning about what services we have available.

By the third day, if the youth decide this is a good program and they want to stay, they can renew their futon for a week by going over to the counseling center. Then they access a counselor and begin to work on a plan.

We're doing these plans on a week-by-week basis because we know these kids are not long-range thinkers. And we know that, if we can get one week's worth of goals with some supportive activities and an adult to assist in getting them done, then we're introducing the kids to the world of planning.

We're hoping that we can help them to begin to prioritize their aims and to find out that there are options out there. We're very anxious to empower these youths and to turn their heads around from the sense that they are victims—which they generally are when they come into this kind of system—to the view that they have some kind of control over their lives. If we can guide them into some responsible decision making, I think that we will be giving them skills that they can take with them. We're not going to be able to stabilize everybody's life through this project, but, if we can teach every kid a little something about how to survive, how to make choices, how to take care of themselves, I think we're going to be planting the seeds for some real good further down the road.

If a youth expresses an interest in family reunification, that is definitely the direction we are going to move. We will be able to do family counseling if the family is local. If not, we will work to prepare the youth for reunification and network with various agencies, such as Travelers Aid, to help a youth get back home. If a youth does not express interest in family reunification, we are not going to pressure in that direction.

Lots of kids that I have dealt with are set on becoming a rock star or a TV personality. One of the most effective ways of working with those kids is to help them experience life's realities. I have a routine line in responding to these aspirations: it may be a little difficult at your age, however, here are the in's and out's of how you get an agent, where you go for auditions; these are trade papers you might want to read—by the way, you need your composite photographs; here's our card in case it doesn't all work out. And, by the way, we also offer shelter and food and other things should you need that.

I draw on my own past experience in the entertainment field. The kids hear the agent part, the industry part, how to get into a union, and they think they have gotten the resource person of the century. Great! I'm delighted that they see me as a resource person and they go tromping out happy as can be about becoming a star. They are back the next day saying, "You know how much composite photos cost?"

And I say, "Yes. They are kind of expensive."

And the kid says, "Well, I don't have that kind of money. I am going to have to get a job."

It is much easier to talk to kids about a job when they have brought it up than if you've brought it up. They remember Dad who said, "If you didn't get that job, you better not come back." We don't want to get on that same track.

So, we let those kids put out their agenda and we go with it—to the degree that makes sense. Chances are we're going to be able at some point to mesh with a realistic plan that the youth is going to be able to shape. That's what we're hoping to do.

Safe House will have a job developer operating full time out of the counseling center to work with organizations within the community and to find entry level jobs for these kids. We also have a special live-in maintenance person. This handy person will be working on not only keeping the facility in shape but also doing weekend projects and renovating things around the place with kids. This will have a twofold purpose. One is to teach them skills, to help them learn how to carry out handiwork. The second is to assess their readiness for jobs and to find out if they are reliable. What are their hang-ups? Do they understand instructions? Can they take supervision? This way, we will be able to provide references for kids who are appropriately ready to go into the job market. We can cite their strong points and specify where they need a little extra supervision. We can help some of the kids make a start in the world of work and also help keep our facility in the best possible shape.

We will have material provisions on the premises. In fact, when a kid comes into the counseling center, we will be asking: Do you need a meal? Do you need some new clothes? Do you want to take a shower? That is how it starts off. Kids can deal with counseling a little better when they are feeling clean and not distracted by hunger. Then we'll start getting to the next level—finding out what's going on in their lives.

We will be able to provide a lot of basic services there and then begin to work out some of the auxiliary services and a stabilization plan. Kids can use the counseling center only if they are using the shelter. That is the key to access into the system. If a kid comes in and just wants some counseling, we will refer them to one of the many agencies that already do that kind of thing. We are trying to hook our services to the shelter to see if a combined, integrated program is a way to get kids off the streets. Some powerful events in their lives brought them there. The cure has to have potency behind it also.

Integrative Analysis:
Individual Level
to Federal Level

CASE IN POINT

(Practitioners Talk About Their Work with Clients)

FRANK

Frank walked into our counseling office extremely angry and hostile. He was sixteen years old, white, and from out of state. He had been living on the streets for some time. Before that he broke away from a residential psychiatric facility. He stated, with a mixture of a snarl and a smile, that he was ready to beat up anyone who messed with him. His urgent request was shelter. Frank came across as a young man with severe emotional problems; it stuck out all over him.

With my encouragement, a mixture of cautious teasing and maternal indulgence, Frank proceeded to spill his story. His birth mom gave him up at an early age, allegedly due to inability to provide for him. He and his sister were placed in a series of foster homes, where he remembers being physically abused. He was adopted by a military family and recounted an extensive stay in Japan. Some problems cropped up in Japan when Frank began having difficulties in school. But the problems intensified when adoptive mom and dad divorced, and mom proceeded to marry a very young stepfather, who didn't get along with Frank. His mom thought it best for Frank to leave, and his stepdad went further and threatened him physically if he didn't. So he left. He stayed for a while with an uncle and aunt, and then a grandmother. By now his school phobia and off-beat habits had intensified greatly, and the family couldn't handle the situation. They had him placed in a psychiatric facility, where he has been for the past year.

When I contacted Mom, she had her own story to tell. Frank had allegedly threatened his sister with a knife once, terrorizing her in the extreme. Mom would not allow me to give Frank her phone number or address. She seemed genuinely frightened of him.

Frank admitted the incident to me, expressed tremendous remorse as a result, and kept begging to be allowed to speak to his sister to apologize. Mom wouldn't permit it! It appeared that some healing time was needed. Frank manifested tremendous despair. He was extremely depressed as a result of this separation and feeling of abandonment. I saw and spoke to Frank daily. He needed a great deal of firm, sustained support to see him through this period.

After Frank got involved (innocently) in an illicit scheme that could have resulted in immense trouble for him, I connected him to a home for mentally deficient males. Frank acquired both his own room and a pet cat. The organization turned out to be very good for him, and he thrived there. His face literally softened; he was no longer the tight, angry kid who had walked in the door originally.

After a time, he agreed to my suggestion to move to a group placement where he could attend an alternative school daily. Luckily, he connected up very positively with one of the teachers. His aversion to school melted away in a short time. Sometimes luck makes more of a difference than all our theories and treatment schemes.

He left placement on his eighteenth birthday, obtained a loan, and decided on his own to attend a security guard school. Graduation was a very special day for him and for me. I took lots of pictures.

Frank is presently nineteen years old, works as a security guard, and lives with a roommate. He wasn't one of my easiest cases. It was touch-and-go there for a time. I still worry about his violent flashes of anger, especially with the job he holds. And his relationship with his mother remains tenuous. She lives out of state, and they talk on the telephone every once in a while. But, when I think back to where he started, I realize that, through one means or another, Frank has come a long way. In a recent conversation, Frank himself attributed it all to having found a substitute mother.

Throughout the previous chapters, a volume of information has been presented on causes and manifestations of adolescent runaway behavior, and approaches to intervention have been suggested. Here, these findings and ideas are reformulated in a more conceptual and sociologically oriented way. Perspectives are offered at different levels of human and social aggregation, from the individual runaway to the national social system. Policy implications at each level are clearly articulated. Up to this point, the discussion has centered around the individual and family, as well as the local system. That is where the runaway problem is manifested and played out. However, there is also a national dimension to this issue, in particular, the role of the federal government in providing broad policy leadership and making necessary resources available locally for coping with the problem. In culminating this analysis, the national level is given a place in the discussion.

The approach taken is to integrate in a coherent way material presented separately from the two sources of information: the synthesis of empirical research and the community survey. That integrated content is analyzed and presented according to the levels of human aggregation as follows: individual and family levels (micro perspective), agency and community levels (local system perspective), and the national level (federal system perspective). The results of the research synthesis and community survey I summarized to highlight the problems at each level, and specific policy recommendations are made.

Because the presentation draws heavily on the previous discussion, bibliographical references are kept to a minimum.

MICRO PERSPECTIVE

In beginning a discussion of micro factors in runaway behavior, it should be noted from the start that this is a complex, multifaceted phenomenon that does not lend itself easily to a one-dimensional analysis. Individual and family aspects are highly interrelated and are intertwined with community and societal influences.

Both the research synthesis and the community survey agree solidly on this point. The research tells us, for example, that there is a wide range of reasons for self-initiated home departure, each having its own implications. Among these are escaping detrimental home conditions, including family breakdown or abuse; parent-child conflict or miscommunication; psychological impairment; seeking to "find oneself"; seeking adventure or independence; and trying to find a more compatible value system. In addition, there are externally imposed reasons, symbolized by the push-out/throwaway nomenclature. Here, youngsters are asked to leave or are "thrown out of the house" because of behavior that is discrepant with the expectations or values of parents. The synthesis suggests additional criteria for subdividing the runaway population, such as degree of school success, existence of peer influences and/or supports, the degree of criminal behavior involved, and the extent to which the individual is committed to "street life."

The experts participating in the survey concur in this view. They distinguish particularly between young people who leave home on their own and those who are coerced to leave or are otherwise eased out. Sexual and/or physical abuse is a major factor in a considerable number of cases. A feeling of being "unwanted" or "not belonging" to the family is prevalent in the population.

There is also consensus across these information sources about the implications of an analysis that recognizes the diversity of the runaway population. Service programs, it is agreed, need to be diverse and to respond to the needs of the various subpopulations. The general position is that no single program or approach can solve this problem. For example, the survey respondents highlight different service requirements for young people who voluntarily leave home and for those who are push-outs. For some, family therapy may be the treatment of choice; for others reunification would be a disaster. The need for multiple and comprehensive service approaches is highlighted in the next section, which takes a broad systems view.

In the discussion under the micro rubric, individual level and family level considerations are treated separately. While there is an artificial element to this, it will be useful for analytical purposes.

The Individual Level

Problems. There is a great deal of consensus in the research literature that runaway and homeless youth carry deep psychological scars with them, considerably more than their teenage counterparts, according to comparative studies. When contrasted with nonrunaways, they have been found to have lower self-esteem, less self-confidence, and more difficulty with interpersonal relations, including a lack of social poise. They feel generally that they have less control of their environments, which perhaps accounts for other findings indicating that they are more likely to be anxious, to be defensive, and to exhibit suicidal tendencies. The runaway group, in a study by Roberts (1982), manifested inadequate problem-solving methods. They attempted to deal with stressful situations by going to sleep, crying, turning to drugs or alcohol, forgetting about major elements in their lives, or attempting suicide. All of these coping strategies involve removing oneself from the situation, rather than confronting it. This pattern of destructive thinking has been labeled "cognitive confusion" by Janus and his associates (1987).

The same overall appraisal was made by community experts in the survey. They described runaways as distressed, alienated, disoriented, in trouble emotionally, and prone to depression and self-destructive behavior, including suicide. As in the research synthesis, poor self-esteem was a term often used to characterize this group, and the designations "psychotic" and "sociopathic" were added to describe some, particularly the long-term street kids. It was the view of community experts that, compared with several years ago, runaways are considerably more emotionally disturbed, out of control, younger, and come from families that are more dysfunctional.

The survey respondents made a point of going beyond the psychological realm to describe runaways. They noted the medical condition of the group and the variety of environmental survival needs that they face. The experts found the health status of runaways poor and their energy level low. Commonly reported ailments include sexually transmitted diseases, alcohol and drug abuse, malnourishment and infections (including gynecological infections), poor hygiene, lice, and scabies. Runaways, it was stated, did not have access to preventive care, especially dental care, as prevention generally requires a stable life circumstance. Other health problems identified included dermatological disorders (particularly in hard-core runaways), family planning, bruises and survival wounds, colds, and tension headaches. Respondents pointed out that physical health depends on the length of time the youth has been out on the streets.

Agency-based respondents described the practical, survival problems of individuals they encountered. These youth needed a residence, schooling, and employment. They also lacked more practical things, such as food, clothing and an I.D. card, without which the possibilities of a job or a suitable school arrangement were nil. Some needed legal advice to help with situations they found themselves in. Others required some type of protection from dangers they encountered, real or imagined.

Policies. The major conclusion of the research synthesis is that runaways need sustained counseling and therapy to improve their self-image, self-confidence, interpersonal relationships, and cognitive functioning. The community experts concurred in this position and suggested some related points. A common theme among the responses was the need for better diagnosis and assessment at initial contact to permit development of a case plan to guide intervention. Given the variation among psychological states, differential diagnosis is a clear imperative.

Specialized counseling was considered critical because most of these troubled youth have multiple problems, and it takes multiple resources to meet their needs. Among activities recommended were expanded street outreach efforts, peer group models, and time-limited family therapy, where appropriate. Several experts emphasized the importance of counseling as a preventive measure that ought to be available to youth and their families before they face a crisis.

In order for effective counseling to take place, the creation of a stable physical and environmental context was advocated. This includes adequate health care, dependable shelter for the young person, and removal of immediate environmental pressures. To the degree that the runaway is not embroiled in a myriad of coping activities related to meals, illness, income, and so on, the individual will have energy available to enter constructively into counseling. Thus, environmental support not only serves as an adjunct to counseling but also provides a valuable service in its own right.

Agencies providing counseling to adolescents need to take into account the previous problematic relationships these young people have had with adults and their strong distrust of authority. Also, teenagers are embroiled with the process of seeking out their own values and establishing a stance of independence. For this reason, the initial stage of engagement may be difficult (Katch, 1988).

An approach that is responsive to these factors is suggested by Baker (1982) and employs the following tenets:

- Responsible independence;
- Purposive interaction;
- Freedom of choice;
- Voluntary participation;
- Trust;
- Informed consent;
- Self-determination;
- Information sharing; and
- Honesty and integrity.

Certain practices are derived from this orientation:

- Have clients participate as much as possible in decisions that impact their lives.
- Demystify information so that clients understand what we are doing and give clients as many tools and skills as possible to work on their own problems.
- Help clients find peer support in their environment.
- Help clients identify how their problems are shared by others to develop a "critical consciousness" from which to act.
- Help clients expose the role that oppression has played in their lives.
- Do not ask clients to adjust to oppressive situations but to try to change these situations.
- Help clients see how guilt, self-blame, and failure prevent people from acting.
- Make clients independent, and make ourselves eventually unnecessary.
- Downplay the role of "worker as expert" and instead play up the role as ally or facilitator.
- Give full respect and appreciation to clients, regardless of how disarming their behavior.

An implementation plan presented by Baker has these components:

1. *Contracting*—whenever possible contracting should be used as a means of securing the working agreement. Concrete goals serve to enhance communication and motivate the client and worker while providing a constant reference point for both. The use of contracting is especially

useful in teaching youth responsibility for self, integrity, independence, and decision making.

2. *Individual Plan*—the use of a plan of action for each individual youth serves to heighten self-esteem, to motivate youth, to show investment by the agency, and to develop involvement of the youth and counselor. During adolescence the search for identity, accompanied by a strong need to be a part of a group, creates ambivalence about what the youth wants or needs. By late adolescence, absolute need for peers should be reduced. The use of the individual plan helps the youth in seeing his or her self as different from the group.

   a. Explore options, choices, and alternatives.
   b. What are the consequences?
   c. What do I want?
   d. How am I going to get it?

3. In working with youth, use easily understood language. Clarity in communications becomes essential in the development and maintenance of a relationship with troubled adolescents. Prior life experiences in which double-bind messages have been the norm may prevent youth from clearly communicating. Often the youth may be "streetwise" but have limited education and language skills. It is important that the worker develop and use with youth:

   a. Active listening skills;
   b. Ownership (teach the youth to take responsibility for self and actions), that is, "I" messages;
   c. Teaming (make the youth a part of the team if in group or individual counseling);
   d. *Talks with* the youth rather than *about* the youth; and
   e. A way in which the youth can develop a sense of humor and use it as a part of the treatment plan.

4. The methods by which the agency operates should be bound by (a) *a sense of firm and just caring* and (b) *consistent limits, boundaries, and expectations*. The worker may use:

   a. Role play and role reversal;
   b. Reality testing;
   c. Peer counseling;
   d. Group counseling;
   e. Problem solving; and
   f. Decision making.

Finally, basic to continuous work with the runaway youth, the counselor should be able to provide values clarification, which includes teaching the adolescent constructive and acceptable use of anger and how to fight fairly. Adolescents should have the freedom to make mistakes and use them as a positive learning experience.

In another counseling and case management program that this author helped to establish and evaluate (Rothman, Furman, Weber, Ayer, & Kaznelson, 1987), direct service to youth included the following components.

Assessment. This is the process in which caseworkers met the adolescent and, through interviews and in-depth discussions, determined the needs of that adolescent and tried to obtain a clear understanding of any environmental factors that precipitated his or her running away. Assessments were basic and were reported in 93 percent of the cases. The small percentage not receiving assessment may have been extremely short-term cases or cases assessed previously by other agencies.

Client and family counseling. Counseling to youth involved crisis intervention, problem solving, planning for employment and independent living, and a range of other interpersonal interventions. Of all the services provided directly, client counseling was the most frequently offered (96 percent of all clients) and was regarded by the counselors as the most important service they provide.

Family counseling, in which family members were asked to come into the program for discussion and resolution of family conflicts, was provided in 57 percent of the cases.

Reunification. Services aimed specifically at reunification of the adolescent with the family were provided in 25 percent of the cases. Reunification was not always the most desirable alternative for a runaway because of family disorganization, physical or sexual abuse, economic hardship, and so forth. In addition, the adolescent may not have been willing or ready to return at the time the family was ready to take the adolescent back.

Food, clothing, and shelter. Provision of food, clothing, and shelter are basic necessities of life, and many of the clients had no means of obtaining these basic requirements. Provision of food was reported in 59 percent of the cases; provision of clothing, in 41 percent of the cases; and provision of shelter, in 59 percent of the cases. While the program itself did not provide shelter, counselors moved a child from shelter to shelter or intervened in his or her living situation to assure the continuation of an appropriate domiciled condition.

Identification. In order to obtain general relief funds, to get a job, or to qualify for placement, an adolescent must have identification. Caseworkers sometimes escorted adolescents to the Department of Motor Vehicles to obtain state identification cards. This service was provided in 12.8 percent of the cases.

Independent living skills. This type of counseling consisted of training adolescents to budget resources, find and maintain housing, and cope effectively with the day-to-day responsibilities of living alone. Preparation for independent living generally took place in cases in which the adolescent was ready to be emancipated. Emancipation was an alternative usually available to the older adolescents around the ages of sixteen and seventeen. This type of counseling occurred in 25 percent of the cases.

Given the troubled circumstances of life confronting most runaway and homeless youth, a circumscribed guidance approach was often not enough to meet client needs. This program was obliged to arrange for co-lateral services from diverse community resources. The referral sources that we tracked in this program included the following ones.

Counseling and individual treatment. This type of counseling refers specifically to long-term or intensive counseling services provided by others after the adolescent is placed in suitable housing. Many runaways require additional counseling to sort through problems. Referrals for individual counseling were reported in 74 percent of the cases.

Family counseling. Family counseling helps runaways and their families to continue on a longer-term basis to work through the confidence that precipitated the adolescents' decision to leave home. Referral for such continued service occurred in 44 percent of the cases.

Housing and placement. Housing and placement referral services include temporary as well as permanent placement. Residential arrangements may involve a group home, foster home, or an institutional setting, such as a drug rehabilitation center or a psychiatric hospital. The family ordinarily attends to these varied needs. In the absence of family sustenance, an array of substitute supports need to be marshalled. This type of referral was provided to somewhat over 50 percent of the cases.

Health service. Referrals for health services generally occur upon initial screening of a client. As part of the assessment, the caseworker determines whether or not any medical or psychiatric services are needed. Such referrals were made in 55 percent of the cases.

Legal services. This referral is made when adolescents come with outstanding warrants or other conflicts with law enforcement agencies. Some 15 percent of the clients required this assistance.

Vocational services. Vocational assistance in seeking and maintaining employment is of critical importance to adolescents who are seeking emancipation from their families. These referrals were made in about 20 percent of the cases.

Educational services. Educational services involve reenrolling runaways in school, either at their original school or at the site of their new placement. It also includes making appropriate referrals for those who want to obtain a high school equivalency certificate in order to qualify for college, as well as for adolescents with various types of learning disabilities. Referrals for educational services were provided in 31 percent of the cases.

Substance abuse services. Substance abuse services are provided for any adolescent who comes to the program with any sort of chemical addiction. Referrals for substance abuse treatments were required in 9 percent of the cases.

Sex information. Sex information involves educating the adolescent about all aspects of sex, including responsible sexual behavior. Females who require contraception are referred to clinics for information and services; those who suspect they are pregnant are referred for appropriate counseling and services. Both sexes are informed about sexually transmitted diseases. Sex information referrals were reported for 26 percent of the cases. This figure should be seen in the context that many of the adolescents came from other agencies that provide information and assistance in this area.

Because of their age and developmental stage, adolescents are highly enmeshed in family life. Families, accordingly, are the context in which problems arise; sometimes they are the cause. In either case, they can be a vital force for support and amelioration.

The Family Level

Problems. There is strong evidence that family factors play a critical role in the runaway phenomenon. Numerous empirical studies and the observations of knowledgeable individuals in communities point to the family as salient in generating runaway behavior. This is not to say that the family is the only stimulus or that all culpability resides in the family, with young people remaining impeccable and blameless in their actions. Indeed, organizations such as Toughlove focus on youthful excesses and urge harsher, more controlling, and more self-protecting ways of reacting by families. The research studied examines the question—"In what ways do family variables contribute to runaway initiatives by adolescents?" Using that as a point of departure, questions of communication, structural disruption, abuse, deviant behavior, and rejection merit discussion.

Communication. Findings identify poor communication as a significant factor in the etiology of departure of youth from their families. On the one hand, parents indicate that runaways do not obey them or cooperate in family expectations, such as coming home on time. On the other hand, young people say that their parents reject them, are uncaring, too strict, do not listen, and are not empathic about their situation. Thus, runaways frequently perceive themselves as being unloved or unwanted by their families. The community experts identified poor communication as a major element in most instances of home departure. They report that, in about three-quarters of the cases, runaways cite communication problems with their parents as the main reason for breaking with the family. Other factors may precede communication problems, such as divorce or marital discord, but such intensified pressures create strained parent-child communication.

Structural Disruption. The community experts considered family disorganization to be the next most important runaway stimulus. They indicated that some 50 percent of the youth they worked with identified factors such as divorce, separation, a new stepparent, blending of families, and the likes as the backdrop for the decision to "split." The research synthesis comes to similar conclusions and provides some elaboration. For example, difficulties may arise if the family is larger than average or if there are many younger siblings. The latter may cause decreased parental attention for the older children and intensified sibling rivalry in search of attention from the parents. Another study discovered that many runaways come from families in which all the other siblings are of the opposite sex. Thus, family structures in which a child feels isolated, neglected, or alienated commonly contribute to adolescent leave taking.

Parental Abuse. A striking finding of the community survey was that some 40 percent of the runaways spoke of physical abuse as a significant factor in their situation, and somewhat over 25 percent made reference to sexual abuse. Apparently, runaways come from homes that often present unbearable environments for young people to grow up in. Several of the research studies note the occurrence of incest between girls and their fathers or father substitutes, typically a stepfather. Thus, contrary to the popular image in some circles of runaways being carefree, irresponsible seekers of adventure and pleasure, the reality is that many are victims escaping from intolerable and extremely destructive home situations.

Maladaptive Family Behavior. Studies indicate that a preponderance of families of runaways manifest behavior that is severely dysfunctional. Parents may be engaged in "deviant" activities of various kinds, including abuse of drugs or alcohol. Some parents may have committed criminal acts or in various ways may be in trouble with the law. It has also been found that the social climate and pattern of interrelationships within the family can contribute to deviant behavior. There may be a high level of conflict, lack of cohesion, confusion over role expectations, and detrimental conditions for personal growth of family members. Some investigators refer to a lack of family orientation, which includes little feeling or belonging to the family, minimal emotional closeness, and inability to adapt to a changing external environment. Tensions between the parents or between a parent and another child may cause one of the more vulnerable or less conforming children to become a scapegoat, diverting attention away from the troubling matter. The survey respondents, concurring in these views, note also that over the recent past, runaways they have been in contact with have come from families showing a discernible increase in such maladaptive and dysfunctional behavior.

Parental Rejection. The matter of parental rejection has been mentioned previously under other rubrics, but it merits additional discussion. Most of the other factors involved in family level problems include an element of parental rejection, directly, as in scapegoating, or indirectly, as in the context of poor communication. Rejection interconnects with the other family problem areas, and indeed none of these factors stands alone; all are highly correlated. The connections among rejection, poor communication, family disruption, and physical abuse were noted by many survey participants. Disrupted families with a single parent or merged families often include the introduction of an unfamiliar adult, most often a stepfather "who tries to take over." Interviewees reported that young females were often rejected and abused by the stepfather or the mother's boyfriend. Physical abuse and more subtle rejection were also specifically related to alcoholism and drug use.

Policy. Many status offenders come from families in which divorce or separation has occurred. Other family problems and dysfunctions may be involved. Often it is not sufficient to deal with the runaway alone. The family must be involved in the search for solutions to the problems. Family-oriented intervention should be given high priority. In various studies, it has been found to reduce recidivism; curtail youth involvement with the juvenile justice system generally; aid families in which traditional social service agency interventions have failed; foster school adjustment; enhance parental self-confidence; encourage greater use of communication resources; and facilitate increased family cohesion.

One of the strongest conclusions emerging from the empirical research synthesis relates to the efficacy of family-oriented intervention in serving status offenders. The beneficial effects of family crisis therapy are recorded in the project evaluations of Baron and Feeney (1973) and Bohnstedt (1978). After nine months of operation, the Sacramento County Diversion Project showed a decline in recidivism rates for runaways and other juvenile status offenders (Baron and Feeney, 1973). A later examination of eleven California juvenile diversion projects found that the three that actually reduced recidivism used specialized family counseling (Bohnstedt, 1978). Similar results were obtained by Beal and Duckro (1977), Stratton (1975), Morgan (1982), Kogan (1980), and Piven (1979).

The significance of family intervention is highlighted in D'Angelo's study (1984) of a "one-shot" interview of families of runaways. He compared families who were seen for one session in a counseling interview with a control group of those who declined to take part in an interview. Families participating in the "one-shot" experience exhibited gains in school adjustment of the children, parental self-confidence, and use of community resources.

The experts in the survey strongly supported family therapy but for only a portion of the client population. Their experience suggests that four distinct service modalities are necessary to provide for four different away-from-home populations. Only 47 percent of the runaways seem to have home environments suitable to return to. Thus several service patterns appear necessary:

1. Family intervention services to facilitate reconciliation and reunion with the natural family *(about half of the clients)*;
2. Substitute facilities, such as a group home or foster care *(close to one-third)*;
3. Preparation for independent living, including help in locating and setting up an apartment, in gaining skills to obtain a job, and in becoming connected to a suitable helping network *(about five percent)*; and
4. Different service offerings, whose character is not altogether clear, for established street dwellers, including medical assistance and food *(about one fifth)*.

A large number of runaways can gain substantially from family counseling, although overreliance on it can be counterproductive.

For those youth who can be reunited with their families, intervention—emphasizing communication and problem-solving training—is most appropriate. Barth (1986: 374–387) outlines a useful process. First, the therapist meets with the youth and family members to encourage them to be open to the idea of restructuring family patterns. Second, the therapist works with the family to assess the specific problems that contribute to the adolescent's runaway behavior and to develop a baseline against which the family's progress can be measured. Third, the family members are taught communication skills for problem solving. Using role playing and other techniques, the counselor helps individual family members learn how to express and to receive appreciation and criticism.

In the fourth stage of therapy—after family members begin to communicate more often and more affirmatively—the counselor helps the family to decide on and to define a particular problem that needs to be tackled. In the fifth stage, the family members discuss, evaluate, and choose possible solutions, taking into consideration both the standard family procedure for dealing with the problem and new and/or ideal solutions. Each solution is then assessed by the family members in terms of its practicality and potential for lessening the problem. Finally, in the sixth stage, the therapist helps the family to implement the preferred solution. Implementation requires steps common to many counseling and behavior modification efforts: planning, task identification and assignment, rehearsal, and repeated effort. This is not the only, or necessarily the best, approach. It does, however, deal with factors related to bringing about family reunification by an outside party when the family itself is incapacitated.

As stated above, for many youth—particularly those who come from highly abusive home environments or who have deep-rooted street lives—a family intervention strategy is inappropriate. For these young people, Barth recommends a rehabilitative approach (1986: 364–365, 393–394). Individual counseling and, if possible, family therapy might still be applied, but the focus shifts toward assisting the youth to develop a stable and independent living situation. Practical instruction is offered in such areas as securing housing, finding work, budgeting, living with roommates, and avoiding substance abuse, combined with assistance in developing "life skills" and support for prosocial behavior. The relative weight accorded to personal versus practical issues in the rehabilitative process depends on the youth's age and social-psychological history; generally, the older and less troubled the youth, the more capable he or she is to prepare for an independent life.

While the need for serving young people at the micro level is compellingly clear, funds for providing the help are appallingly lacking. A recent General Accounting Office (GAO) report, while calling for increased emphasis on outreach activities and aftercare (U.S. General Accounting Office, 1983: 22–23), stops short of recommending additional allocations, suggesting instead that runaway and homeless youth shelters be provided with "more guidance" on these issues. Yet sensitive consultation alone will not enable agencies to expand their services unless new resources are brought into play. Indeed, when GAO asked center staff and other community service providers to list the weaknesses of the runaway and homeless youth programs, "inadequate funding" topped the list, followed by three other funding-related issues: limited shelter space, inadequate staff, and limited experience and training of some staff members. The amount of additional resources needed varies among programs, but ideally each agency should receive enough added support to hire a full-time outreach worker, as well as a competent counseling staff of sufficient size to conduct long-term individual and family therapy within the program or to arrange for such care through referral to another facility. Organizational and community policies and programs obviously are instrumental in the provision of services to individuals and families. They provide both the context and the mechanisms for service delivery.

LOCAL SYSTEM PERSPECTIVE

System variables inherent in human service organizations and the local community must be considered along with personal and family factors in attempting to understand the dynamics of adolescent runaway behavior. As noted in Chapter 1, prior to 1974 many runaways were labeled status offenders and placed in closed detention. This policy met with opposition from a coalition of civil libertarians and children's rights advocates, who sought to restrict the powers of the juvenile courts and to extend legal protections to the young; fiscal conservatives, who wanted to spend less money on costly services; and the hard-liners, who wanted to reduce the frills provided to marginally troublesome youth and devote the majority of resources to detaining dangerous delinquents. The Juvenile Justice and Delinquency Prevention Act of 1974 reflected the interests of this diverse coalition through the federal government's policy of deinstitutionalization.

Deinstitutionalization removed the problem of runaway and homeless youth from the juvenile justice system. Since many youth have valid reasons for escaping their family environments—and are often in critical need of psychological support and counseling—there is no benefit in dealing with them as though they were criminals. Unfortunately, the alternative mechanism for serving the runaway population—the multiple community agencies funded by and large under the Runaway and Homeless Youth Act—generally have been unable to handle the number of young people who need assistance or to provide the intensive and sustained intervention that they require. Responsibility is no longer fixed and centralized in the courts, as it was before the act. Deinstitutionalization has resulted in dismantling of accountability. Consequently, as experts polled in the Los Angeles County survey observed, many runaway and homeless youth simply wander about making sporatic contact with the service network.

The Organizational Level

Problems. The research synthesis led to the firm conclusion that no single program or strategic approach has been associated with effective outcomes for assisting runaways. The problem of runaways is a complex phenomenon with many dimensions, which requires different policy initiatives. Perhaps not enough is known about the phenomenon or about approaches for dealing with it (Kobrin and Klein, 1982). Insufficient funds and inadequate and/or insufficiently trained staff have impeded the development of successful programs.

A National Academy of Science report (Linney, 1982) found considerable variation in the quality of programs and no consensus among professionals on the best service modalities. Indeed, agency staff members were found to be dispirited and "hopeless" about their work situation and discouraged about funding cuts, program retrenchment, rapid staff turnover, and restrictive licensing requirements in temporary shelters.

The community experts expressed similar views. The vast majority felt little or nothing was being done to help runaways adequately. They described staff members as either overburdened or limited by resource deficits and legal restrictions.

There was a sense that the prospects for runaways are questionable, both emotionally and financially. Future employment prospects are poor because of some of the types of problems (alcohol and drug abuse) involved. Many of the respondents observed that status offenders lacked education, resulting in limited employment prospects. The outlook is bleak according to some, because there is no service continuity, only emergency, short-term assistance.

When the experts were asked to indicate the agencies and services they considered to be doing excellent work in the community, there was no agreement. This underscores the absence of a firm basis for designing programs for runaways.

The service pattern in the community was characterized as "patchwork." Only a very small number of agencies had an "open-door policy" and a wide range of services to all youth who approached them. The majority had narrow program definitions, leading to fragmented, specialized services and the rejection of service requests made by many young people. Service was refused for many reasons. In some situations, primarily the shelters, there was simply a lack of beds. In other cases, the agency that the youth approached was inappropriate; for example, the service desired was not available (long-term care, hospitalization, or suicide counseling).

Frequently, an agency accepts referrals from only one main source, for example, the police. Sometimes service was refused because the youth exhibited symptoms of substance abuse (high or intoxicated), possessed a weapon, sought to hustle or deal drugs, or refused to give sufficient personal information. Agencies that turn down requests make referrals to other agencies and may offer transportation.

By and large, local informed observers reinforced broader research findings and supplemented these through elaboration and examples.

Policies. The community experts recommended that local organizations exercise greater commitment to the problem of runaways and to the age group in general by cooperating with other agencies, making a greater effort to overcome turf and communication problems, being less competitive about funding, and seeking to use all available resources.

Greater commitment means also expending more time, money, and effort. Agencies were urged to do all they could to expand their services. A frequently cited mechanism for accomplishing this was the use of contracts between voluntary and public agencies. In this way, packages of funds could be allocated to agencies with the facilities to meet certain needs.

Those interviewed said that agencies should become more visible about their services; cooperate with law enforcement; work more with grass-roots groups; employ better management procedures; serve more hard-to-place clients; offer more residential programs; develop more transitional living facilities; and provide more long-term treatment.

An array of agency services were identified, suggesting the scope of programmatic possibilities: individual, group, family, crisis intervention, and hot-line counseling; referrals to shelters and social services; food, clothing, shelter, and medical services; legal and advocacy services; job development and vocational training; basic survival skills training; tutoring and special education; and cultural and recreation activities.

In the discussion of shelter, long-term placement received special emphasis. Federal programs provide mainly immediate, emergency aid. Long-term shelter is a pressing need, however, because about one-half of the runaway population cannot return to the family environment. Long-term or transitional care is expensive. In a period of economic stringency, many communities have simply turned away from dwelling with the issue of long-term care. It is clearly a salient area for policy development.

It is easier to describe the range of services than to enumerate the impactive ones. Research lends little insight and parallels exactly the conclusions of the community leaders reported earlier. Returning to the comment by Clark, Ringwalt, and Ciminello (1985: 27): "There is no substantial accumulation of evidence to support the efficacy of any treatment or service." However, some particular services in given locales have been found to be effective.

The Children's Aid Society of New York provided parent-child mediation services over a three-year period in four boroughs of New York City, bringing young people and their parents together to discuss their difficulties. Volunteer mediators played conflict-resolving roles. Mediation between parents and children was found to be effective in three-quarters of the cases. A Wayne County, Michigan, juvenile diversion program placed participants in individually tailored multimodal treatment plans, based on client need. Community services, youth service center resources, and counseling services were combined in an individualized plan, with positive effects. Another study concluded that a limited range of clearly targeted services achieved favorable results. Environmentally oriented support, including vocational counseling and training, academic counseling, and tutoring, was found in another study to be particularly successful. Programs that emphasize physical fitness have also produced measurable benefits.

It appears that effective programs incorporate several components in an integrated design. For example, combining advocacy with psychological guidance in a juvenile diversion program had a positive effect on recidivist behavior. Thus, a policy direction is suggested by terms such as targeting, individualizing, integrating, orchestrating, mediating, and combining. A mixture of approaches tailored to specific client needs seems desirable.

There was clear consensus in the research synthesis and the survey of experts that achieving strong programs requires able staff. The research pointed to the use of competent, well-trained staff as an aid to effective and cost efficient service delivery. In a study of juvenile correctional programs, Greenwood (1982) concluded that the variable chiefly associated with program effectiveness was quality of staff. Conversely, the lack of adequate staff was found to inhibit the provision of meaningful services (Bolton and Brown, 1978). The kinds of skills needed have been discussed in many studies and can be summarized as follows: the ability to recognize the conflicting views of involved parties; the ability to understand the nature and extent of authority, how to use it, and how to collaborate with it; the ability to question; and the ability to use adversarial and mediating techniques.

The research also noted positive results in using volunteers in staff support roles. College students seem to perform especially well in a volunteer capacity, perhaps because of their position in the life course, midway between adolescence and adulthood. They can identify sympathetically with youth, yet bring some measure of maturity to the situation. Tasks especially suited for volunteers included vocational assistance, academic tutoring, counseling, and advocacy.

Staff training and development also received priority mention among the survey participants. Many thought personnel lacked the expertise and attitudes needed for helping youth. Specific job performance requirements included the ability to use authority appropriately when dealing with adolescents and to respond sympathetically to youth who behave in a deviant and provocative fashion.

The Community Level

Problems. In its investigation of status offender services, the National Academy of Sciences study (Handler and Zatz, 1982) highlighted a number of community level issues. Following deinstitutionalization, no particular format or pattern for dealing with status offenders emerged in American communities. Responsibility had moved from the correctional system to the social system, but the new arrangement exhibited "widespread variation." Many youth were "being ignored altogether." A discernible proportion failed to meet the requirements of any particular agency and thus remained deprived of needed services.

Furthermore, agencies functioned in autonomous and idiosyncratic ways and did not coalesce into an articulated human service network. The research found that the agencies showed "minimal evidence of community integration."

The community experts surveyed were especially vocal on this matter and illustrated the problem in various ways. Unanimously, they cited poor communication and coordination among service agencies. They observed turf problems, competition for funds, and minimal information sharing. Many pointed to a very large information gap between the public and private sectors and attributed some of the difficulty to heavy staff workloads.

Beyond this broad issue of service interrelationships, the research synthesis isolated another important system defect. There appears to be no identifiable point of entry into the service system, no agreed upon professional locus for assessing a person's problem and making rational decisions about how the array of services may be brought to a particular case. Research on juvenile court dispositions tells us that, apparently, the point of intake into the service system substantially conditions the kinds of treatment status offenders receive. Decisions about disposition and service often are made in irrelevant, discriminatory, nondiagnostic ways. Intake decisions are shaped by such factors as race and ethnicity, class, gender, and presence of a parent or a lawyer.

Some studies correlate disposition decisions to specific personal attributes. Black adolescent offenders draw more severe treatment because of their dress and demeanor, and urban youth are dealt with more severely than some rural youth. Females are held in custody longer and are allocated less average time for their disposition than males. Although they commit less serious offenses, more girls than boys are held in detention. The courts and the police explain the discrepancy by claiming that girls need protection for their safety.

A young female's sexual activity is viewed as self-destructive and as a sign of personal, familial, and emotional problems, while male heterosexual behavior is viewed more liberally and is taken less seriously. Typically, male behavior is defined in terms of aggressive acting out with society rather than as a manifestation of deeper disturbance. As a result, females are more likely to be given an out-of-home placement, while males are more likely to be allowed to remain in their own homes.

The survey group expanded upon these community variables from several standpoints. Respondents particularly emphasized the lack of community understanding and commitment as a major obstacle to confronting the runaway problem. This attitude results in part from confusion and disquiet about teenage behavior. As a group, adolescents are not viewed sympathetically by the majority population. The experts participating in the survey also noted the following community level problems exacerbating the runaway phenomenon: breaking down of the family; lack of parental responsibility; a diverse runaway and homeless population; and inadequate legislative statutes.

Policies. When it came to suggesting policy recommendations at the community level, survey respondents were unified in advocating greater cooperation and communication among agencies. They felt that purposive planning and synchronized coordination were essential for raising the level of service for needy youth, and they emphasized the need for transforming what may be a hodgepodge of services into a coherent service delivery system.

Survey respondents called for establishing a central point of intake. As a centralized information and referral body, such an agency would establish guidelines for defining the categories of status offenders and the kinds of services needed by each; would coordinate pickup, detention, assessment, and treatment; and, by making maximum use of existing community resources, would refer clients to the appropriate service provider.

The group of experts also recommended the development of policies to promote community-based *prevention*. Areas identified for preventive work were diverse and included interaction between the parents, pupil, and teacher in the schools; parenting education; early intervention in schools, churches, and neighborhood networks and organizations; public education; and advocacy training.

Schools. School personnel have daily contact with children and interact with many parents. As the only adult nonfamily members who see children regularly, teachers are able to identify emerging problems before they become critical, to communicate with parents, and to assist in referring families to professional help.

Parenting Education. Parenting education programs may be helpful to both intact and single-parent families, and can address areas such as self-esteem, coping, decision making, communication, developmental factors, and parental control.

Early Intervention in Schools. Early in-school intervention is based on the view that status offender problems begin in the primary grades. Teaching decision-making skills at the primary level can help to prevent such problems as sexual abuse. Peer support can be encouraged, with young children serving as a resource for one another.

Natural Helping Networks. Natural helping systems, such as churches, neighborhood organizations, after-school programs, drop-in centers, the YMCA or YWCA, and family service agencies, offer to youth and adults opportunities for dialogue and ventilation. A communitywide approach is necessary to handle adequately the problems caused by the stresses experienced by many families.

Public Education. Programs are needed to increase public awareness of the problems of youth. Mass media, as well as face-to-face encounters, such as discussion groups and workshops, may be effective.

Advocacy. Advocacy carries public education a step further. It may mean providing specific moral or material support for specific young people or lobbying for (or against) specific legislation.

Any effort to assist runaway and homeless youth must recognize sociocultural processes in the community that place some young people at risk. These include social influences in school, the neighborhood, and the work world that are responsible for rejecting and stigmatizing youth (Brennan, Huizinga, and Elliot, 1978: 83–84). Preventive policies need to consider eliminating negative labeling and opening up access to positive social roles, such as productive work opportunities, meaningful participation in community affairs, engaging in institutional decisions at school, and so on. Policies need to create situations that make youth feel that they are integral to the pattern of life within both the family and the community.

While there is agreement in the field that a stable environment is essential for psychological aid to be effective, there is a sharp division concerning secure detention as a way to deliver therapeutic and other services to the individual. Some professionals favor a form of secure detention as a means of initiating a treatment process, with two limitations. First, detention would be a short-term experience, so that youth would not languish in secure detention; second, detention would be utilized only with a limited sector of the status offender population, the small percentage of youth who are drastically out of control. Other professionals strongly oppose secure detention, seeing status offenders strictly as victims in need of voluntary community-based services.

The question of secure detention for status offenders is perhaps the most divisive issue at the local level and probably the most troubling aftermath of the 1974 Juvenile Justice federal legislation. These who favor detention, including school personnel, law inforcement officials, juvenile justice officials, and service providers from both the public and private sectors, claim that limited detention facilitates the start of a diagnosis and treatment process, showing runaways that someone cares enough to give them a structure. Detention's advocates see it as a short-term, limited approach that serves as a platform for referral to helpful programs. They object to the term "lock-up" because it does not convey the notion of providing help. Some of the professionals decry the fact that legal authority was taken from them by the deinstitutionalization legislation, leaving them without legal or programmatic "teeth" as a tool for engaging a volatile and often intractable but terribly needy client group.

Almost all detention advocates stress the need for special treatment resources for status offenders and the requirement that they clearly be separated from juvenile and adult offenders in a special place resembling a "boarding school with a fence," "something homelike . . . not punishment." Under such involuntary residential conditions, it is argued, runaways would receive needed counseling and reconciliation services, and parents would also, in a stable environment, receive the support and assistance they need to handle their children's problems.

Other professionals vigorously oppose detention for youth. Their position is that the status offender runaway does not belong in the criminal justice system, as many are victims rather than offenders. Those eschewing secure detention believe it carries with it an inherent potential for abuse. Once detention is allowed, they observe, it becomes a crutch to be used with a multitude of individuals, including those to whom it does not apply at all. They liken detention to opening Pandora's box—some use leads inevitably to overuse.

The answer, they contend, is provision of a sufficient range of community services to provide assistance on an intensive basis. In this way, the artificial and potentially damaging mechanism of forced detention will not have to be brought into play.

The question of secure detention as an aid or detriment to providing counseling and other support services to troubled youth is a highly contentious, unsettled one. It constitutes a key policy issue whose resolution merits concerted, immediate attention.

FEDERAL SYSTEM PERSPECTIVE

National Level

The national level was not part of the initial study that underlies this book. Because of the significance of federal influence, however, the national level is included in this summary analysis. The federal government is largely responsible for developing broad macro policy and for shaping service delivery toward runaway and homeless youth. State and local governments in many parts of the country also play a role, but the most significant legislation—along with the preponderance of funding—originates in Washington, D.C.

Problems. Basic federal policy is set by the Runaway and Homeless Youth Act, which authorizes the Secretary of Health and Human Services to provide support to state and local governments, profit and nonprofit agencies, private entities, and coordinated networks of these agencies dealing with the immediate problems of runaway youth and their families. Programs funded by the Act are micro oriented. They are designed to alleviate the problems of the runaway youth population; reunite children with their families and encourage resolution of intrafamily problems through counseling and other services; strengthen family relationships and create stable living conditions for youth; and help youths decide on a future course of action for their lives (U.S. Department of Health and Human Services, 1985: 3).

The total appropriation for the Runaway and Homeless Youth Act in fiscal year 1985 was $23,250,000. Of this amount, $18,128,766 was awarded to 273 runaway and homeless youth programs, with an average grant of $68,865 to refunded programs and $39,674 to new programs. Approximately $718,000 was awarded to 13 coordinated networks that provide support to all the programs, and $350,000 was allocated for the National Runaway Switchboard, which provides referral and crisis intervention services to youth and their families via telephone. The remaining $2,900,000 was awarded to research and demonstration projects (U.S. Department of Health and Human Services, 1985: 5–21).

The number of youth who made use of these federally funded services during fiscal year 1985 was substantial. The Department of Health and Human Services (HHS) reports that 67,800 youth were provided shelter or ongoing services, and another 274,000 youth received crisis intervention or other assistance on a drop-in basis. The National Runaway Switchboard logged approximately 260,000 calls, over one-half of which came from runaway youth who had been away from home for at least four days (Department of Health and Human Services, 1985: 9,21).

Despite the apparently positive trend indicated by these figures, there are substantial problems and difficulties in these national programs. If there are more than 1,000,000 runaways and 500,000 homeless youth, federally funded programs are serving perhaps one-fifth of the eligible population. Yet there does not seem to be any evidence that shelters are turning away youth due to lack of bed space.

One explanation is that all youth who want services are receiving them, with others returning to their families or eschewing agencies. The more likely possibility, however, is that federally funded runaway programs are not making an adequate outreach effort. Perhaps because shelter can only be provided to a few, agencies find it in their best interests to limit their marketing and publicity; otherwise, they would be inundated by needy young people. One survey of 215 runaway youth in Los Angeles and San Francisco—including 124 youth identified by social service agencies and 91 recruited off the streets—found that less than 20 percent knew of any shelters that served runaways (Miller et al., 1980: 70–71). These young people were somewhat familiar with the social service system; nearly one-half, for example, knew that free medical clinics were available. That so few were aware of shelters suggests that runaway programs did not adequately publicize their availability. A 1983 GAO study of seventeen federally funded shelters found that, while centers utilized standard publicity techniques (advertisements, speeches, and contact with school officials), they engaged in minimal outreach activity on the streets (U.S. General Accounting Office 1983: 22).

With respect to services for those youth who have program contact, most agencies are prepared to deal with immediate crisis. Very few are equipped to provide long-term intervention or follow-up, as noted in the Los Angeles County community survey. One survey of 139 runaway youth in Colorado found that only 10 to 15 percent of those who had stayed in runaway shelters received services of any kind after returning home (Brennan, Huizinga, and Elliot, 1978: 321). In the GAO study, agency staff at twelve of the seventeen shelters estimated that less than one-half of the youth received any aftercare, and, among those who did, the service was most often limited to a single session of family counseling (U.S. General Accounting Office, 1983: 13). Given the intense family and personal problems experienced by many runaway and homeless youth, the scarcity of aftercare appears to be a glaring shortcoming of federal service delivery policy.

In this light, the accomplishments of the nationally sponsored runaway and homeless youth shelters are subject to question. HHS notes proudly that, in fiscal year 1985, 52 percent of the youth who received ongoing services at HHS-funded shelters were reunited with their parents (U.S. Department of Health and

Human Services, 1985: 17). However, if little or no aftercare was provided, there is no way of knowing whether these reunifications lasted or whether reunification was a wise course to take.

As Moses (1978) points out, the weaknesses of the programs that were operated under the federal Runaway Youth Act[1] are not surprising, given its legislative history. When the act was passed in 1974, it mirrored the existing runaway house model: the 1960s "crash pad" that served the more or less "normal" youth. Such a youth might be a fourteen-year-old middle-class girl who has been gone for three or four days and then returns home without police intervention. Of course, some runaways today still fit this picture, but most are more seriously troubled (Moses, 1978: 229). It is unlikely that a "quick fix" program model will cope satisfactorily with these severe problems. Yet federal policy embraces little else. Illustratively, Killeen (1986) points out that provisions in United States legislation are below those offered through the Home Persons Act in Great Britain.

Policies. Runaway and homeless youth issues may be seen as a subset of the problems of a larger, unstable youth population. What is lacking and desperately needed is a national policy—a youth policy—that broadly addresses child and adolescent needs and develops resources on their behalf. Such a policy would build upon existing systems that serve youth but would unify these services under the banner of providing protection and opportunity for children and adolescents. At a minimum, a national youth policy would provide an adequate level of funding, encourage program coherence, designate fixed responsibility for service delivery, and offer or induce specific needed services. From a broader social perspective, a preventive policy would:

1. Provide full and fair employment opportunities for all families in order to provide a firm economic base in which youth may develop. Families are the fastest growing segment of the homeless population (Edelman and Mihaly, 1989).
2. Diversify academic programs and increase support services within the schools to meet the intellectual and personal needs of students with a broad range of capabilities, needs, and backgrounds. Many youth do not have the educational and vocational skills to succeed (Crystal, 1986).
3. Develop more employment, recreational, and participation opportunities to channel youth's energy in positive directions and enhance their ability to make current contributions and future transitions to the work world. It has been noted that direct job creation programs need to accompany job readiness services (Abbott and Blake, 1988).

---

[1] The Runaway Youth Act was renamed the Runaway and Homeless Youth Act by Congress in 1980.

4. Increase the availability of community mental health services to enable youth and families to detect emerging problems early and to function at their optimum level. Many families need assistance to facilitate intergenerational communication (Kufeldt and Nimmo, 1987; Kammer and Schmidt, 1987).

5. Strengthen the capacity of child protective services to intervene in abusive family situations and to provide quality foster care when necessary. Victims of child abuse may suffer severe psychic consequences, including evidence of posttraumatic stress syndrome (McCormack, Burgess, and Hartman, 1988).

6. Strengthen current child care programs and make them more responsive to the needs and perspectives of youth. Because of existing deficiencies, a high incidence of runaway behavior is reported from institutions ostensibly established to serve adolescents (Speck, Ginther, and Helton, 1988; Price, Chaffee, and Constock, 1986; Hirschberg et al., 1988). In a similar vein, it is important to enhance those programs in the child care system that prepare youth for independent living. Currently, a high proportion of the graduates of these programs join the homeless (Raychaba, 1989).

The problems facing many of the nation's youth cannot be viewed in discrete terms; neither should the policy options be viewed in narrow, categorical terms. The objective of a national youth policy is to begin addressing the problems and solutions more comprehensively. Multiple, flexible, and broad-ranged policy and program initiatives are necessary to address diverse problem conditions (Van der Ploeg, 1989; Schulman and Kende, 1988).

The Children's Defense Fund, a research and lobbying organization headquartered in Washington, D.C., has produced a "Children's Survival Bill" that might serve as a rallying point for youth policy advocates (Children's Defense Fund, 1985: 71–78). The bill proposes a legislative agenda for children, adolescents, and families, building on existing federal programs for troubled youth and families. It recommends, for instance, that the current appropriation for the Runaway and Homeless Youth Act be doubled. In addition, it suggests specific developments and improvements in the nation's child care facilities, prenatal and health care services, educational systems, food and nutrition programs, income support system, tax laws, and employment and training programs. The details can be found in the model bill. The Children's Defense Fund estimates that these enhancements would require increased federal spending above the present allocations for youth and family services.

In the face of staggering federal deficits, the prospect of securing substantial new funding seems dim. Consequently, the Children's Defense Fund bill outlines a plan for reduced military spending and increased tax levies to finance the expansion. What is far more convincing, however, is the evidence that the Children's Defense Fund provides on the cost effectiveness of the programs in the long run. Simply stated, youth who are not integrated into their families or their communities often extract from society a great deal more dollars in the future. It costs $12,000 per year to house an inmate in prison, for example, and $16,000 per year to provide institutionalized care for a foster child (Children's Defense Fund, 1985: 71). It is wiser—and more humane—to intervene before these kinds of responses become necessary.

To place the Children's Defense Fund bill on the national agenda requires a vigorous education and lobbying effort by those who know and work with youth: social workers, educators, and, of course, parents. People must start talking more openly and more forcefully about the many problems and issues of the young and about the costs of continued neglect.

Until the nation places a higher priority on the welfare of its youth, the prospects for significant improvement in the lives of the runaways and the homeless remain dim. It is trite to claim that an investment in youth is an investment in the nation's future, but it is also true. Whole populations of young people are being ignored, neglected, and, in a sense, abused by their society. Is that any less serious or alarming than child abuse inflicted by a single family?

GETTING ORGANIZED

(Administrators Talk About Their Agencies)

THE NATIONAL NETWORK OF RUNAWAY AND YOUTH SERVICES

The National Network is a group of over 700 community-based agencies that share an interest in helping troubled youth and their families. The Network was begun by over fifty representatives of alternative youth programs from across the nation. That was in 1974. These programs had a commitment to experiment with new ways of providing services to young people who had largely "turned off" to mainstream social agencies and had been turned away by many of them.

The success of these new local programs was quickly evident, but it was also evident that they lacked the resources to sustain and expand their work. The Network immediately began promoting the service models that were being delivered in local communities. It soon became a prime example of the power of grass-roots organizing.

The Network has become a strong advocacy organization, with members in each state. It is a nonprofit organization, governed by a seventeen-member board representing ten regions, special interest caucuses, and youth. There is a nationally elected chairperson to coordinate the board's activities.

We are a strong voice expressing the needs and viewpoints of the youth that its members serve. Through grass-roots advocacy, we communicate with elected and appointed officials. Our group has successfully advocated for such things as increased funding for the Runaway and Homeless Youth Act, improved legislation for high-risk youth, and deinstitutionalization.

We have encouraged steps toward the creation of a national youth policy, something vitally needed to unify all factions working with young people. The Network has been instrumental in the creation of a national committee to work on a Younger Americans Act.

Advocacy skills of members are developed at the Network's annual symposium, in which participants conduct hearings on important issues, debating and defending their viewpoints in an effort to have their positions officially adopted by the Network. Resolutions that are posed are taken to Congress, where we sponsor "Hill Day." This is a designated time when Network members from across the country build congressional relationships and disseminate the Network's position on legislative issues to key elected representatives.

Once legislation is adopted, the Network works with the appropriate federal agency, educating the members of the agency and monitoring implementation of the legislation. As we have sharpened our advocacy skills, we have applied them to the state and local levels. For example, we were instrumental in the creation of state children's trust funds, state runaway and homeless youth acts, and legislation separating juvenile and adult offenders.

Network members relate their advocacy success to the effectiveness of the Network's public education programs. We have been instrumental in bringing the plight of runaway, homeless, and "throwaway" youth into the public's consciousness. By developing close working relationships with media people on the national level, we have generated television appearances by Network staff and members on such programs as *Donahue, Hour Magazine, Today, CBS Evening News,* and *Canada AM.* We have also placed printed articles in such newspapers as the *Wall Street Journal, New York Times,* and *Washington Post.*

We have worked out relationships with the press on all levels. Frequently, board and staff members have been responsible for connecting the national press with local organizations. And local programs make a point of referring inquiring journalists to the national office for more expanded or technical information. Some of our most powerful public education messages have come from well-known groups and individuals who have taken up our cause. The Network assisted Larry Gatlin and the Gatlin Brothers on their hit record, "Runaway Go Home." And now Starship has become a national spokesgroup for our organization, providing a distinctive vehicle for reaching the youth at risk who need our help.

We use this same approach to create public service announcements that are for the exclusive use of member agencies. New World Video, which owns the "Streetwise" video distribution rights, has produced a powerful television spot. And Bruce Weitz of *Hill Street Blues* has made two public service announcements—one talking to youth and one to potential supporters of the Network and the National Fund.

Our organization sponsors and conducts research projects examining alternative youth service programs. We collaborate frequently with other organizations interested in the same kind of work, including federal agencies. One of our most effective methods of working with the federal government is through setting goals and policies. The Network, together with its members, creates a prioritized list of areas requiring research and demonstration and presents this list to government officials. Many of our suggested ideas get incorporated into federal initiatives.

We also do research on our own, both locally and nationally. The study "To Whom Do They Belong?" was sponsored by National Fund money and created by volunteer Network members. Our documentation of the incidence of youth homelessness has been widely referenced and used by members of Congress and many national organizations. In addition to doing its own research, the Network has been active in funding demonstration projects through its member agencies.

A major project is the National Fund, which provides long-term financial stability for both advocacy efforts and direct services. The National Fund was started in 1982 as a result of Dotson Rader's cover stories in *Parade* magazine. Since then, hundreds of people have sent donations to the Fund and requested information on how to get involved. The money is put to effective use by the staff and volunteers of the Network. For example, the Fund covered the printing and mailing costs of "To Whom Do They Belong? A Profile of America's Runaway and Homeless Youth." This report was done entirely on volunteer time, with the Fund underwriting direct expenses. The report has been praised for helping policymakers and funding sources hammer out responsible decisions at the federal, state, and local levels. In addition, in a more direct way, the Fund has clothed, fed, counseled, and sheltered hundreds of youth through its grants to runaway youth programs.

Our program from its beginning has had a firm commitment to youth participation. We define youth participation as the active involvement of young people in the design and delivery of services provided by youth services agencies. Members are encouraged to develop activities that promote youth empowerment, responsibility, and productivity through the use of the creative energies of youth. We believe that youth-adult partnerships are vital to finding fundamental solutions to the problems of youth and that, when troubled youth are excluded from decisions that affect their lives, it increases their apathy and hopelessness. There are youth members on the National Network Board of Directors. They have given vital leadership to efforts by state and regional networks and local agencies to bring young people into decision-making roles. We are an organization that bases its operations on wide participation. It isn't enough to be effective. We want to be democratic at the same time.

Research Methodologies

METHODOLOGY USED FOR RESEARCH SYNTHESIS

The literature search was conducted through computerized retrieval techniques, with the assistance of information science experts at the UCLA Graduate School of Library and Information Science and the University Research Library. Six computerized data bases identified as fundamental for this study were thoroughly scrutinized:

- Dissertation Abstracts
- ERIC (Educational Resources Information Centers)
- Mental Health Abstracts
- National Crime Justice Reference Service
- Psychological Abstracts
- Sociological Abstracts

These data bases were selected to cut across varied and differing sources of literature.

Through a preliminary review of the literature and preliminary piloting of the data bases, the following set of key words and descriptors was delineated for guiding the search:

Alternatives to institutionalization	Deinstitutionalization
Crime	Delinquents (Delinquency)

Diversion programs   Juvenile status offenders
Homeless youth   Runaways
Juvenile code offenses   Status offenders
Juvenile delinquents   Truants
Juvenile justice   Ungovernable juveniles
Juvenile Justice and Delinquency   Wayward youth
   Prevention Act   Youth service bureaus

Through these procedures, some 851 published items (journal articles, research reports and monographs, books) were retrieved. Added to this were reports, books, and monographs known to the staff outside formal search procedures. The staff reviewed each item, sifted out the empirical work, and coded it into eleven different categories. The code sheet contained the following categories:

Client Data
   1. Characteristics of status offenders (age, sex, class, ethnicity, family structure, personality, etc.)
   2. Type of status offender
      a. Runaway
      b. Sexual activity
      c. Drug use
      d. Truancy
      e. Disobedience (incorrigibility)
   3. Comparison studies (compared with delinquents, with nonoffenders)
   4. Recidivism rates and patterns
   5. Escalation

Program Data
   6. Approaches and Strategies
   7. Programs and practices
   8. Court intervention
   9. Deinstitutionalization
   10. Needs

Only the items coded as empirical research were reviewed. Each item was assessed in terms of gross criteria of research adequacy. When a study failed to meet obvious standards of methodological adequacy, such as sample size, representativeness, or indication of explicit research procedures, it was eliminated. Approximately 100 studies constituted the data pool for this portion of the study.

The research team worked with computerized abstracts when these were complete and adequate. When they were not, or when supplemental information was necessary or useful, the full article was reviewed. Other articles or books that came to the attention of the team were also included in the information base. Abstracts restrict the amount of information available in the pooled studies, but they have the advantage of assembling a large aggregation of study results within a given time period for making generalizations. Nonetheless, use of abstracts is a limitation and needs to be kept in mind by the reader in appraising the conclusions and recommendations.

All the studies were examined within their categories. Studies treating an identical subarea (such as programs) were grouped together. Generalizations were made based on a consensus in findings among different researchers studying different samples in different settings. A convergence of results among disparate investigators was the basis for forming specific generalization. In every instance, policy, program, or practice implications were extrapolated from each generalization, so that the action guidelines are close to the data and represent clear, logical applications of the generalizations. (For a description of the technique, see Rothman, 1978, 1980 and Mullen, 1978.)

METHODOLOGY USED FOR SURVEY OF LOS ANGELES COUNTY KNOWLEDGEABLE INDIVIDUALS

This survey constituted a form of needs assessment. According to the needs assessment research literature (Warheit et al., 1984), there are five methods of conducting a needs study:

1. Interviewing key informants through a survey
2. Holding a large community meeting or forum in which information is given by participants
3. Gathering information from service-providing agencies about rates-under-treatment of their clientele
4. Using available statistical data as social indicators
5. Conducting a field study of the population along the lines of a broad public opinion poll

Each of these approaches has advantages and disadvantages, and rarely, if ever, are all of them employed simultaneously. In this case, the first method was followed as the primary approach because of the advantages enumerated by Warheit and his associates. The method is relatively simple and inexpensive to administer; it permits the input of many different individuals; it encourages a broad discussion of needs and services of importance to the community; it establishes lines of communication among community actors; it generates enthusiasm; and it fosters "a more concerted community-based approach to the establishment of priorities and the allocation of resources" (Warheit, 1984: 42). Thus, the method at the same time provides for data gathering and initiates a process for taking action.

The disadvantages of the method are also discussed by Warheit: the expert informants "are not representative of the community in a statistical probability sense" and hence may overlook the views or needs of some segments of the population. The experts may not provide a precise picture of the totality of types of needs in the community.

In this study, an attempt has been made to compensate for this limitation by reaching out to a wide cross-section of interests and views. The perspectives of the clients themselves—members of the runaway and homeless youth population—have also been included. These are the experts talking about their own situation and needs. Nevertheless, readers should be aware of the methodological constraints on the information obtained and the recommendations derived from it. The survey results were later integrated with empirical knowledge from the literature.

Rates-Under-Treatment

A modified rates-under-treatment method (item 3 above) was also incorporated into the survey. All major agencies providing services to runaway and homeless youth were included in the panel of informants. The survey collected information from each agency about services offered, their volume, the characteristics of the clientele, and problems encountered in providing services. Although the information collected was somewhat uneven because of different degrees and forms of statistical record keeping by the organizations, some objective information about the service pattern in Los Angeles County was collected.

Sample

The experts who were selected as the panel of informants are deeply involved in diverse ways in dealing with runaway and homeless youth, as well as other status offenders, in Los Angeles County. Two groups of runaway and homeless youth (eight in all) were also interviewed.

The panel was assembled by a snowball technique. An original list of experts was compiled by the staff of Department of Children's Services (DCS) after they consulted with professionals in the field. Those nominated were then asked to nominate others. The staff of the Bush Program in Child and Family Policy at the University of California, Los Angeles, employed a paralled snowball procedure by starting with a long-term experienced professional and a scholar-researcher with extensive local community experience and then asking these two experts for nominations. Those nominated were then asked to name others.

The two lists constructed in this way were merged. Those experts who received multiple nominations were automatically included in the final panel. Among the others, choices were made by the staff using the dual criteria of number of nominations and breadth of organizational representation.

The final sample comprised all the major agencies and organizations providing services to runaway and homeless youth, including short-term shelters, group homes, residential treatment facilities, outreach agencies, health providers, hot-line operators, Probation Department officers and administrators, judges, law enforcement officials, school district personnel, coordinating and planning agency representatives, DCS staff, and others with miscellaneous relevant roles and functions. A total of forty-two persons was included, reflecting twenty-nine different agencies and organizations. This included thirty-four adult knowledge-ables and eight runaway youth. Some interviews were conducted in groups in the agency. In a few instances, more than one representative from an agency was included in the tabulations because that person reflected a clearly different level or geographic locale or perspective within the organization. The number of responses varied for any given question. See Appendix C for a list of the panel members and their organizational affiliations.

Clients were asked to provide information about the same problem, as well as their recommendations for action. These were runaway or homeless youth associated with agencies: in one instance, an organization focusing on short-term runaways, and, in the other, on long-term runaways. The young people were interviewed in voluntary groups, each lasting between sixty and ninety minutes. An appropriately modified form of the questionnaire was used. These responses, treated independently rather than integrated into those of the panel, are introduced at appropriate points in the discussion.

Purposive sampling guided the construction of the panel and the approach to reaching youth informants. This is sampling based on rational, logical criteria for selecting respondents, rather than on standard probability techniques. Research specialists advocate the use of this method in appropriate circumstances. Babbie (1973: 106), for example, prescribes the use of purposive or judgmental sampling as follows:

> Occasionally, it may be appropriate for the researcher to select his sample on the basis of his own knowledge of the population, its elements, and the nature of his research aims. . . . In some instances, the researcher may wish to study a small subset of a larger population in which many members of the subset are easily identified but the enumeration of all would be nearly impossible. For example, he might want to study the leadership of a student protest movement; many of the leaders are easily visible, but it would not be feasible to define and sample all leaders. In studying all or a sample of the most visible leaders, he may collect data sufficient for his purposes.

The Questionnaire

The questionnaire was a semistructured instrument with both open-ended and checklisted items. Interviews were conducted in person and ordinarily lasted for between one and two hours. The questionnaire was mailed to the respondents in advance so that they could prepare their answers and the agency could obtain or compile the statistical data requested. The project staff felt that the advantage of having ample time to reflect on the subject outweighed the disadvantages of biased or contrived responses. It also enabled the staff to conduct the interviews within the short time available.

The questionnaire was organized into several parts. The first nine questions sought objective information about the characteristics of the population and patterns of service provided to them. The next six questions (questions 10–15) dealt with planning and issues—for example, "what place does secure detention have in the treatment of status offenders?" "Should they be considered a single population or various subpopulations for planning purposes?" "Is there sufficient coordination and communication among service-providing agencies?"

The third section (questions 16–20) asked for recommendations to deal with the problem, including what DCS specifically should do, what other community agencies should do, what geographic areas should receive additional service, what programmatic approaches should be given priority, and what types of preventive measures should be taken. See Appendix B for the text of the questionnaire. The presentation of results does not precisely follow the order of the questionnaire schedule.

The questionnaire was pretested with two respondents—one from the private sector and one from the public sector. Based on these experiences, it was revised in several ways. To train interviewers, one of the interviews was conducted by the project director and observed by four staff members who were members of the survey project team. The group then thoroughly analyzed the interview. This collective interview and subsequent discussion ensured a standardized approach among different interviewers. Established procedures were also formalized, put in writing, and thoroughly discussed by the group. For example, these were the guidelines for interviews:

- Write as much as necessary during the interview but not more.
- Do the final write-up as soon as possible after the interview.
- Obtain word-for-word quotations whenever someone makes a particularly striking or clarifying remark.
- Keep the interview on track, while allowing room for flexible responses.

The following standard format for introducing the interview was established:

Give your name, then identify the three groups sponsoring and collaborating in the study. Tell the interviewee that the study will focus on the status offender problem and runaway youth. *Status offender* is broadly defined for the purpose of the study, but it will also emphasize runaways. Then explain why the interviewee was selected to be interviewed. Explain that there will be specific program recommendations coming from the study, and there will be an opportunity for community response and input about the recommendations. Finally, tell the interviewee that a follow-up stage of field testing and evaluation programs is planned. Assure the individual that responses are confidential. Explain that a report of results and recommendations will be sent to all respondents. The questionnaire is long, so tell the interviewee to give his or her impressions and move on rather than answer questions in depth. Then ask the interviewee to follow along as you read the items.

In the telephone conversation in which the appointment is arranged, interviewers were asked to mention that the first seven questions call for factual estimates, so it would help if data and reports are taken from the files beforehand in instances where the organization is a service provider.

Data Analysis

The mode of analysis was simple and straightforward. Quantitative items were hand tabulated, and extensive use was made of the means and range in analyzing responses. Quantitative measures involved identifying basic concepts or themes inductively from the open-ended responses, coding all responses within these categories, and then quantifying these in terms of means. The quotations are as exact as possible in representing the thoughts and specific words of the panel members, but, because of the length and complexity of the interviews, these comments may not be absolutely identical to the original language. The reader should be aware of this potential minor discrepancy. The study is primarily qualitative in character, and this quantification of results was not emphasized.

Survey Questionnaire

UNIVERSITY OF CALIFORNIA, LOS ANGELES
SCHOOL OF SOCIAL WELFARE
Bush Program in Child and Family Policy

JUVENILE STATUS OFFENDER SURVEY

Date of interview _____

Interviewee _____

Title _____

Organization _____

Phone Number _____

Interviewer _____

General comments on the interview:

Did the interviewee suggest any other possible interview subjects? If so, please list names, organizational affiliations, and phone numbers.

Characteristics of the Status Offender Population

1. How many status offenders does your agency/office serve in the course of a year?

   Are there perceptible seasonal variations, or is it more of a steady flow?

   Can you give me a breakdown of this number by type of service offered?

   How many kids do you turn away in the course of a year and for what reason?

   Of the kids you serve
   What percentage have been "pushed out" of their homes by their families?

   What percentage are: _____ from within L.A. County

   _____ from outside L.A. County

   _____ from outside California

   What percentage would you estimate are repeats to your agency?

   What percentage would you estimate have had prior involvement with other social service agencies?

2. Can you give me an estimate of the size of the total juvenile status offender population in the county? On what do you base that estimate?

3. Do you serve a particular subgroup of the status offender population?

4. Of the kids you see, what percentage say they are running away because of the following? Can you corroborate these complaints? (If so, check.)

Percentage Complaints   Corroborate

_____   _____ Communication difficulties with parents

_____   _____ Family disruption (divorce/separation)

_____   _____ Physical abuse at home

_____   _____ Sexual abuse at home

_____   _____ Wants to be on his/her own by choice

_____   _____ Other

5. In general, how would you characterize the health and mental status of the status offenders you see or know about?

What percentage would you estimate have the following problems? Of those, what percentage require specialized treatment? (Enter in parentheses.)

_( )_ Drug abuse   _( )_ Physical health

_( )_ Alcohol abuse   _( )_ Pregnancy

_( )_ Psychiatric   _( )_ Other

6. What percentage of the kids you are currently seeing

_____ Have a realistic prospect of returning home

_____ Have a realistic prospect for successful substitute or out-of-home placement

_____ Are ready for emancipation

_____ Are sophisticated, streetwise kids who are living on their own

7. Has the population you're seeing changed over the past few years?

    _____ Yes _____ No If yes, in what ways (e.g., age, ethnicity, offense?)

8. What is the typical "career" of the kids you see (e.g., Where do they come from before you see them? Where do they go after they leave you? What are their long-term prospects?)? Is it possible to generalize?

9. What effect do you feel your organization has had on this "career trajectory?"

ISSUES

10. Should status offenders be considered one population for planning purposes, or should specific needs of particular subpopulations (e.g., ethnicity, age, sexual preference, type of offense) be addressed?

    _____ One population _____ Subpopulations (Please explain.)

11. In your view, what's currently happening to status offenders in L.A. County?

12. What are the main programs and services currently available to them? How adequate are they? (List services and rate on a four-point scale below.)

Program Service   Adequacy

	Poor	Fair	Good	Excellent
_____	1	2	3	4
_____	1	2	3	4
_____	1	2	3	4
_____	1	2	3	4
_____	1	2	3	4
_____	1	2	3	4

13. To what degree is there communication and coordination among these agencies and programs in the county? If there are gaps, where are they most critical?

14. Since the Dixon bill prohibited secure detention of status offenders, local governments have markedly decreased their involvement with this population, leaving the major responsibility for them with the private sector. What can we learn (if anything) from our pre-Dixon bill experience about how to deal with these kids?

15. Are you aware of exemplary programs or service delivery models locally or in other areas whose experience we could benefit from?

ACTIONS

16. In your view, what are the main stumbling blocks to improvement of our local response to juvenile status offenders?

17. Are there communities (geographic or population) in the county that are particularly underserved with respect to resources for juvenile status offenders?

18. What, if anything, should be done to address the issue of status offenders?

    By the Department of Children's Services?

    By other groups (e.g., private agencies) in the county?

    At the state level?

    At the federal level?

19. As you may know, the county Department of Children's Services is now beginning to look at vulnerable children who in the past have been characterized as status offenders. Given that, which of the following should be the *top priority* for DCS and why?

    _____ Specialized counseling resources

    _____ Emergency shelter beds (e.g., SODA)

    _____ Long-term placement options for "hard-to-place" kids

    _____ Secure placement options

    _____ Other

20. What can be done in the area of long-term prevention of runaway and other status offenses?

21. Is there someone else you feel we should talk to who could add to our understanding of this issue?

A P P E N D I X   C

Participants in the Survey of Community Experts

Community-Based Organizations

Aviva Center	Executive Director
Aviva Respite Center	Director
Angel's Flight	Director
Children of the Night	Executive Director
	Intake Coordinator and Outreach Supervisor
Hollywood Community Services (Options House)	Program Director
Homeless Youth Project	Program Director
High Risk Youth Project (Children's Hospital and L.A. Free Clinic)	Co-Director
Gay and Lesbian Community Services Center	Interim Director, Housing and Youth Department
John Rossi Youth Foundation	Executive Director
Juvenile Justice Connection Project	Executive Director
Penny Lane	Assistant Executive Director
Rosemary Cottage	Executive Director
1736 Project	Executive Director
South Bay Juvenile Diversion Program	Executive Director

149

Teen Canteen (Traveler's Aid Society)	Executive Director
Tough Love (Parent Support Group)	Founder-Director; Advisor

Government and Other Organizations

California Council on Children and Youth	Executive Director
INFOLINE	Executive Director
Los Angeles County Department of Children's Services	Division Chief, MacLaren Children's Center
Los Angeles County Department of Community and Senior Citizens Services	Project Supervisor
Los Angeles County Office of Education (Attendance and Administrative Services)	Assistant Director
Los Angeles County Probation Department	Chief Probation Officer Director, Central Placement Office
Los Angeles County Sheriff's Department	Director of Youth Services Bureau
Los Angeles Police Department	Juvenile Division Aide
Los Angeles Superior Court	Presiding Judge, Juvenile Court Supervising Judge, Dependency Departments Juvenile Court Coordinator, Delinquency
Los Angeles Unified School District (Pupil Services and Attendance, Senior High Division)	Coordinator
Pasadena Police Department	Youth Services Coordinator
Status Offender Detention Alternatives Program (SODA), Los Angeles County Probation Department	Deputy Probation Officer
Van Nuys Superior Court	Judge

Bibliography

Abbott, M. L., and Blake, G. F. 1988. An intervention model for homeless youth. *Clinical Sociology Review, 6,* 148–158.

Adams, G. R., and Munro, G. 1979. Portrait of the North American runaway: A critical review. *Journal of Youth and Adolescence, 8*(3), 359–373.

Adams, G. R., Gullotta, T., and Clancy, M. A. 1985. Homeless adolescents: A descriptive study of similarities and differences between runaways and throwaways. *Adolescence, 20*(79), 715–724.

Aptekar, L. 1989. The psychology of Colombian street children. *International Journal of Health Services, 19*(2), 295–310.

Babbie, E. R. 1973. *Survey research methods.* Belmont, Calif.: Wadsworth Publishing Company.

Baker, C. 1982. "Working with adolescents: the changing scene." Region VI Child Welfare Training Center, Tulane University.

Baron, R., and Feeney, F. 1973. Preventing delinquency through diversion: The Sacramento County 601 diversion project. *Federal Probation, 37*(1), 13–18.

Barth, Richard P. 1986. *Social and cognitive treatment of children and adolescents.* San Francisco: Jossey-Bass.

Bartollas, C. 1975. Runaways at the training institution in central Ohio. *Canadian Journal of Criminology and Corrections, 17*(3), 221–225.

Bauer, M., Bordeaux, G., Cole, J., Davidson, W. S., Mitchell, C., Singleton, D., and Martinez, A. 1980. Diversion program for juvenile offenders: The experience of Ingham County, Michigan. *Juvenile and Family Court Journal, 31*(3), 53–62.

Beal, D., and Duckro, P. 1977. Family counseling as an alternative to legal action for the juvenile status offender. *Journal of Marriage and Family Counseling, 3*(1), 77–81.

Berg, I., Butler, A., Hullin, R., Smith, R., and Tryer, S. 1978. Features of children taken to juvenile court for failure to attend school. *Psychological Medicine, 8*(3), 447–453.

Binder, A., and Newkirk, M. 1977. Program to extend police service capability. *Crime Prevention Review, 4*, 26–32.

Blakely, C. H. 1981. The diversion of juvenile delinquents: A first step toward the dissemination of a successful innovation. Doctoral dissertation, Michigan State University, East Lansing.

Blood, L., and D'Angelo, R. 1974. A progress research report on value issues in conflict between runaways and their parents. *Journal of Marriage and the Family, 36*(3), 486–491.

Bohnstedt, M. 1978. Answers to three questions about juvenile diversion. *Journal of Research in Crime and Delinquency, 15*(1), 109–123.

Boisvert, M. J., and Wells, R. 1980. Toward a rational policy on status offenders. *Social Work, 25*(3), 230–234.

Boisvert, M. J., Kenney, H. J., and Kvaraceus, W. C. 1976. Massachusetts deinstitutionalization: Data on one community-based answer. *Juvenile Justice, 27*(2), 35–40.

Bolton, W. D., and Brown, D. W. 1978. *Rural juvenile delinquency: Problems and needs in East Tennessee.* Knoxville: Institute of Agriculture, University of Tennessee.

Brennan, T., Huizinga, D., and Elliot, D. S. 1978. *The social psychology of runaways.* Lexington, Mass.: Lexington Books.

Brothers, C. L. 1986. The Gestalt theory of healthy aggression in beyond-control youth. *Psychotherapy, 23*(4), 578–585.

Byles, J. A. 1980. Adolescent girls in need of protection. *American Journal of Orthopsychiatry, 50*(2), 264–278.

Caton, C. L. 1986. The homeless experience in adolescent years. *New Directions for Mental Health Services, 30*, 63–70.

Chambers, C., Grinnell, R. M., and Gorsuch, R. L. 1980. Factors associated with police and probation/court dispositioning: A research note. *Journal of Sociology and Social Welfare, 7*(2), 246–258.

Chapin, G. 1978. Heartbreak kids. *Washington Post Magazine*, 12 November, pp. 10–13, 15–16.

Children's Defense Fund. 1985. *A children's defense budget: An analysis of the President's FY 1986 budget and children.* Washington, D.C.: Children's Defense Fund.

Clarke, S. H., and Koch, G. G. 1980. Juvenile court: Therapy or crime control, and do lawyers make a difference? *Law and Society Review, 14*(2), 263–308.

Clarke, S. H., Ringwalt, C. L., and Ciminello, A. H. 1985. *Perspectives on juvenile status offenders: A report to the North Carolina Governor's Crime Commission.* Chapel Hill, N.C.: Institute of Government, University of North Carolina.

Collingwood, T. R., and Engelsgjerd, M. 1977. Physical fitness, physical activity and delinquency. *Journal of Physical Education and Recreation, 48*(6), 23.

Collingwood, T. R., Williams, H., and Douds, A. 1976. HRD (Human Resource Development) approach to police diversion for juvenile offenders. *Personnel and Guidance Journal, 54*(8), 435–438.

Crystal, S. 1986. Psychosocial rehabilitation and homeless youth. *Psychosocial Rehabilitation Journal, 10*(2), 15–21.

Curry, J. F., Autry, B., and Harris, H. J. 1980. Structural family assessment with status offenders. *Corrective and Social Psychiatry and Journal of Behavior Technology, Methods and Therapy, 26*(2), 39–44.

D'Angelo, R. 1984. Effects coincident with the presence and absence of a one-shot interview directed at families of runaways. *Journal of Social Service Research, 8*(1), 71–81.

Daley, M. R. 1983. Social work advocacy in the juvenile court: An exploration study of interventive strategies. Doctoral dissertation, University of Wisconsin, Madison.

Daly, M., and Wilson, M. 1985. Child abuse and other risks of not living with both parents. *Ethnology and Sociobiology, 6*(4), 97–210.

Datesman, S. K., and Scarpitti, F. R. 1975. Female delinquency and broken homes: A reassessment. *Criminology, 13*(1), 33–55.

Denno, D. J. 1980. Impact of a youth service center: Does diversion work? *Criminology, 18*(3), 347–362.

Denoff, M. S. 1987. Cognitive appraisal in three forms of adolescent maladjustment. *Social Casework, 68*(10), 579–588.

Denoff, M. S. 1987. Irrational beliefs as predictors of adolescent drug abuse and running away. *Journal of Clinical Psychology, 43*(3), 412–423.

Druckman, J. M. 1979. A family-oriented policy and treatment program for female juvenile status offenders. *Journal of Marriage and the Family, 41*(3), 627–636.

Dunford, F. W., and Brennan, T. 1976. A taxonomy of runaway youth. *Social Service Review, 50*(3), 457–470.

Duryee, M. A. 1980. Development of a family therapist: Training in an interethnic deinstitutionalization-of-status-offenders agency. Doctoral dissertation, Wright Institute, Chicago.

Edelman, M. W., and Mihaly, L. 1989. Homeless families and the housing crisis in the United States. *Children and Youth Services Review, 11*(1), 91–108.

Educational Systems Corporation. 1978. *Development of a typology and the identification of service needs of runaway youth unable or unwilling to return to their family setting.* Washington, D.C.: Educational Systems Corporation.

Englander, S. W. 1984. Some self-reported correlates of runaway behavior in adolescent females. *Journal of Consulting and Clinical Psychology, 52*(3), 484–485.

English, A. 1989. AIDS testing and epidemiology for youth: Recommendations of the work group. *Journal of Adolescent Health Care, 10*(3), 52–57.

English, C. J. 1973. Leaving home: A typology of runaways. *Trans-Action, 10*(5), 22–24.

Erickson, M. L. 1979. Some empirical questions concerning the current revolution in juvenile justice. In L. T. Empey (Ed.), *Future of childhood and juvenile justice.* Charlottesville: University of Virginia Press.

Ferran, E., and Sabatini, A. 1985. Homeless youth: The New York experience. *International Journal of Family Psychiatry, 6*(2), 117–128.

Garlock, Peter D. 1979. "Wayward" Children and the law, 1820–1900: The genesis of the status offense jurisdiction of the juvenile court. *Georgia Law Review 13*(2), 341–447.

Geller, G. R. 1981. Streaming of males and females in the juvenile justice system. Doctoral dissertation, University of Toronto.

Gilbert, G. R. 1977. Alternative routes: A diversion project in the juvenile justice system. *Evaluation Quarterly, 1*(2), 301–318.

Grala, C., and McCauley, C. 1976. Counseling truants back to school: Motivation combined with a program for action. *Journal of Counseling Psychology, 23*(2), 166–169.

Greenwood, P. W. 1982. *The organization of state level juvenile correction programs: Working draft*. Santa Monica, Calif.: Rand Corporation.

Grinnell, R. M., and Loftis, M. 1977. The runaway youth. *Journal of Sociology and Social Welfare, 4*(7), 1122–1131.

Gruher, M. 1979. Family counseling and the status offender. *Juvenile and Family Court Journal, 30*(1), 23–27.

Gullotta, T. P. 1978. Runaway: Reality or myth. *Adolescence, 13*(52), 543–549.

Handler, J. F., and Zatz, J. (Eds.). 1982. *Neither angels nor thieves: Studies in deinstitutionalization of status offenders*. Washington, D.C.: National Academy Press.

Haro, C. M. 1977. Truant and low-achieving Chicano student perceptions in the high school social system. *Aztlan: International Journal of Chicano Studies Research, 8*, 99–131.

Harris, J. 1982. The effect of paraprofessional counselor-client matching on rearrest in a youthful offenders' pretrial diversion program. Doctoral dissertation, Columbia University Teachers College, New York.

Hartman, C. R., Burgess, A. W., and McCormack, A. 1987. Pathways and cycles of runaways: A model for understanding repetitive runaway behavior. *Hospital and Community Psychiatry, 38*(3), 292–299.

Hayeslip, D. W. 1979. Impact of defense attorney presence on juvenile court dispositions. *Juvenile and Family Court Journal, 30*(1), 9–15.

Heck, C. L. 1980. Facility effects on status offender recidivism. Doctoral dissertation, University of Southern California, Los Angeles.

Hersch, P. 1988. Coming of age on city streets. *Psychology Today, 22*(1), 28–37.

Hirschberg, D. L., Masi, E., Harrington, E., Kelley, R., et al. 1988. Summary of the workshop: Why they run from treatment and what we can do. *Journal of Child Care*, 49–57.

Hough, M. 1977. Police cautioning. *Research Bulletin, 4*, 1–4.

James, K. L. 1977. Incest: The teenager's perspective. *Psychotherapy: Theory, Research and Practice, 14*(2), 146–155.

Janus, M. D., Burgess, A. W., and McCormack, A. 1987. *Adolescent runaways: Causes and consequences*. Lexington, Mass.: Lexington Books.

Janus, M. D., Burgess, A. W., and McCormack, A. 1987. Histories of sexual abuse in adolescent male runaways. *Adolescence, 22*, 405–417.

Jenkins, R. L. 1971. The runaway reaction. *American Journal of Psychiatry, 128*(2), 168–173.

Johns, D., and Bottcher, J. 1980. *AB 3121 impact evaluation: Final report*. Sacramento: California Youth Authority.

Johnson, N. S., and Peck, R. 1978. Sibship composition and the adolescent runaway phenomenon. *Journal of Youth and Adolescence, 7*(3), 301–305.

Jones, L. P. 1988. A typology of adolescent runaways. *Child and Adolescent Social Work Journal, 5*(1), 16–29.

Kahn, M. W., Lewis, J., and Galvez, E. 1974. An evaluation study of a group therapy procedure with reservation adolescent Indians. *Psychotherapy: Theory, Research and Practice, 11*(3), 239–242.

Kammer, P., and Schmidt, D. 1987. Counseling runaway adolescents. *School Counselor, 35*(2), 149–154.

Katch, M. 1988. Acting out adolescents: the engagement process. *Child and Adolescent Social Work Journal, 5*(1), 30–40.

Kelley, T. M., Kiyak, A. H., and Blak, R. A. 1979. Effectiveness of college student companion therapists with predelinquent youths. *Journal of Police Science and Administration*, 7(2), 186–195.

Kelley, T. M., Schulman, J. L., and Lynch, K. 1976. Decentralized intake and diversion: The juvenile court's link to the Youth Service Bureau. *Juvenile Justice*, 27(1), 3–11.

Kessler, C. C., and Wieland, J. 1970. Experimental study of risk-taking behavior in runaway girls. *Psychological Reports*, 26(3), 810.

Killeen, D. 1986. The young runaways. *New Society*, 75, 1203.

Kobrin, S., and Klein, M. W. 1982. *National evaluation of the deinstitutionalization of status offender programs*. Vols. 1 and 2. Washington, D.C.: United States Department of Justice.

Kogan, L. 1980. A family systems perspective on status offenders. *Juvenile and Family Court Journal*, 31(2), 49–53.

Kohn, M., and Sugarman, N. 1978. Characteristics of families coming to the family court on PINS petitions. *Psychiatric Quarterly*, 50(1), 37–43.

Kratcoski, P. C. 1974. Differential treatment of delinquent boys and girls in juvenile court. *Child Welfare*, 53(1), 16–22.

Kufeldt, K., and Nimmo, M. 1987. Youth on the street: Abuse and neglect in the eighties. *Journal of Child Abuse and Neglect*, 11(4), 531–543.

Kufeldt, K., and Nimmo, M. 1987. Kids on the street—they have something to say: Survey of runaway and homeless youth. *Journal of Child Care*, 3(2), 53–61.

Labin, S. N. 1980. Interpreting societal reactions: The case of a police diversion project. *Society for the Study of Social Problems*, 1980 Conference.

LaPlante, J. 1977. Diversion: Its importance on the community level. *Deviance et Societe*, 1(4), 459–470.

Larson, J. H., and Roll, D. L. 1977. *A study in disparity between theoretical and operational conceptualization of juvenile diversion*. Grand Forks: University of North Dakota, Midwest Sociological Society.

Latina, J. C., and Schembera, J. L. 1976. Volunteer homes for status offenders: An alternative to detention. *Federal Probation*, 40(4), 45–49.

Leone, P. E. (ed.), *Understanding Troubled and Troubling Youth*. Newbury Park: Sage Publications, 1990.

Leone, P. E., Walter, M. B., and Wolford, B. I. "Toward Integrated Responses to Troubling Behavior," in Leone, P. E., *op. cit*, pp. 290–98.

Lerman, Paul 1980. Trends and issues in the deinstitutionalization of youths in trouble. *Crime and Delinquency*, 26(3), 281–298.

Levine, R. S., Metzendorf, D., and VanBoskirk, K. 1986. Runaway and throwaway youth: A case for early intervention with truants. *Social Work in Education*, 8(2), 93–106.

Levinson, B. M., and Mezei, H. 1970. Self-concepts and ideal-self concepts of runaway youths: Counseling implications. *Psychological Reports*, 26(3), 871–874.

Lewis, M. R., and Hess, H. 1981. Juvenile status offenders: What factors influence their treatment? *State Court Journal*, 5(2), 26–35.

Linney, J. A. 1982. Alternative facilities for youth in trouble: Descriptive analysis of a strategically selected sample. In J. Handler and J. Zatz (Eds.), *Neither angels nor thieves: Studies in deinstitutionalization of status offenders*. Washington, D.C.: National Academy Press.

Little, L. F., and Thompson, R. 1983. Truancy: How parents and teachers contribute. *School Counselor, 30*(4), 285–291.

Loeb, R. C., Burke, T. A., and Boglarsky, C. 1986. A large-scale comparison of perspectives on parenting between teenage runaways and nonrunaways. *Adolescence, 21*(84), 921–930.

Luna, C. C. 1987. Welcome to my nightmare: The graffiti of homeless youth. *Society, 24*, 73–78.

McAndrews, M. M. 1986. Outreach therapy in human service networks: Rationale and case study. Doctoral dissertation, University of Massachusetts.

McCarthy, P. T. 1981. Child welfare workers and the dilemma of adolescent noncriminal behavioral problems: Practice decisions as public policy. Doctoral dissertation, Bryn Mawr College, Graduate School of Social Work and Social Research, Bryn Mawr, Pa.

McCormack, A., Burgess, A. W., and Hartman, C. 1988. Familial abuse & post-traumatic stress disorder. *Journal of Traumatic Stress, 1*(2), 231–242.

McCormack, A., Janus, M. D., and Burgess, A. W. 1986. Runaway youths and sexual victimization: Gender differences in an adolescent runaway population. *Child Abuse and Neglect, 10*(3), 387–395.

McMullen, R. J. 1986. Youth prostitution: A balance of power? *International Journal of Offender Therapy and Comparative Criminology, 30*(3), 237–244.

Mack, J. W. 1969. The juvenile court. *Harvard Law Review, 23*, 104–122.

Mann, C. R. 1976. The juvenile female in the judicial process. Doctoral dissertation, University of Illinois at Chicago Circle.

———. 1979. Differential treatment between runaway boys and girls in juvenile court. *Juvenile and Family Court Journal, 20*(2), 37–48.

———. 1980. Courtroom observations of extra-legal factors in the juvenile court dispositions of runaway boys: A field study. *Juvenile and Family Court Journal, 31*(4), 43–52.

Mathews, L. J., and Ilon, L. 1980. Becoming a chronic runaway: The effects of race and family in Hawaii. *Family Relations, 29*(3), 404–409.

Michaels, K. W., and Green, R. H. 1979. A child welfare agency project: Therapy for families of status offenders. *Child Welfare, 58*(3), 216–220.

Miller, D., Miller, D., Hoffman, F., and Duggan, R. 1980. *Runaways: Illegal aliens in their own land*. New York: Praeger.

Miller, S. A. 1981. Identifying characteristics of truant students. Doctoral dissertation, Lehigh University, Bethlehem, Pa.

Mitchell, C. M. 1980. Nonprofessionals working with delinquent youth: An experimental comparison of university, community college and community nonprofessionals. Doctoral dissertation, Michigan State University, East Lansing.

Morgan, O. J. 1982. Runaways: Jurisdiction, dynamics, and treatment. *Journal of Marital and Family Therapy, 8*(1), 121–127.

Moses, Anne B. 1978. The Runaway Youth Act: Paradoxes of reform. *Social Service Review, 52* (June).

Mullen, E. J. 1978. The construction of personal models for effective practice: A method for utilizing research findings to guide social interventions. *Journal of Social Service Research, 2*(1), 45–63.

Murphy, D. L. 1983. Conflicting perspectives: A situational analysis of attitudes and motivations held by significant actors within the juvenile justice system. Doctoral dissertation, Syracuse University, Syracuse, N.Y.

Murray, J. P. 1982. *Status offenders: A sourcebook.* Boys Town, Neb.: Boys Town Center.

National Network of Runaway and Youth Services. 1985. *To whom do they belong: A profile of America's runaway and homeless youth and the programs that help them.* Washington, D.C.: The National Network of Runaway and Youth Services.

Nelson, G. M. 1982. Services to status offenders and delinquents under Title XX. *Social Work, 27*(4), 348–353.

Nielsen, A., and Gerber, D. 1979. Psychological aspects of truancy in early adolescence. *Adolescence, 14*(54), 313–326.

Opinion Research Corporation. 1976. *National statistical survey on runaway youth.* Princeton, N.J.

Palmer, T. 1979. Juvenile diversion: When and for whom? *California Youth Authority Quarterly, 32*(3), 14–20.

Pietropinto, A. 1985. Runaway children. *Medical Aspects of Human Sexuality, 19*(8), 175–189.

Piven, H. 1979. The status offender controversy: Charges and study evidence. *Child Welfare, 58*(8), 485–499.

Platt, A. M. 1970. *The child savers: The invention of delinquency.* Chicago: University of Chicago Press.

Polivka, L., Eccles, P., and Miller, E. T. 1979. Removal of status offenders from the juvenile justice system: The Florida experience. *Child Welfare, 58*(3), 177–186.

Price, S. B., Chaffee, F., and Comstock, C. 1986. Comprehensive clinical incident monitoring. *Residential Group Care and Treatment, 3*(3), 37–52.

Price, V. A. 1989. Characteristics and needs of Boston street youth: One agency's response. *Children and Youth Services Review, 11*(1), 75–90.

Quay, H. C., and Love, C. T. 1977. The effect of a juvenile diversion program on rearrests. *Criminal Justice and Behavior, 4*(4), 377–396.

Raychaba, B. 1989. Canadian youth in care: Leaving care to be on our own with no direction from home. *Children and Youth Services Review, 11*(1), 61–73.

Reilly, P. P. 1978. What makes adolescent girls flee from their homes? *Clinical Pediatrics, 17*(12), 886–893.

Ritter, B. 1989. Abuse of the adolescent. *New York State Journal of Medicine, 89*(3), 156–158.

Roberts, Albert R. 1982. Stress and coping patterns among adolescent runaways. *Journal of Social Service Research,* 5 (1–2).

Rothman, D. 1971. *The discovery of the asylum: Social order and disorder in the New Republic.* Boston: Little, Brown.

Rothman, J. 1978. Conversion and design in the research utilization process. *Journal of Social Service Research, 2*(1), 117–131.

———. 1980. *Social R & D: Research and development in the human services.* Englewood Cliffs, N.J.: Prentice-Hall.

Rothman, J., Furman, W. M., Weber, J., Ayer, D. M., and Kaznelson, D. 1987. An interim evaluation of the runaway adolescent pilot program. Center for Child and Family Policy Studies, School of Social Welfare, University of California, Los Angeles.

Runaway Youth Act, July 27, 1972, 92nd Congress, 2nd session, Senate Report, 92-1002.

Ryerson, Ellen. *The best-laid plans: America's juvenile court experiment.* New York: Hill & Wang, 1978.

Saccuzzo, D. P., and Milligan, J. R. 1973. Mass truancy hearings: A follow-up study. *Juvenile Justice, 24*(3), 31–40.

Sarri, R. C. 1978. *Adolescent status offenders: A national problem.* In A. Kadushin (Ed.), *Child welfare strategy in the coming years.* Washington, D.C.: U.S. Department of Health, Education and Welfare, Office of Human Development Services, Children's Bureau.

Schlossman, S. L. 1977. *Love and the American Delinquent: The theory and practice of "progressive" juvenile justice, 1825–1900.* Chicago: University of Chicago Press.

Schulman, R., and Kende, B. 1988. A study of runaways from a short-term diagnostic center. *Residential Treatment for Children and Youth, 5*(4), 11–31.

Shane, P. G. 1989. Changing patterns among homeless and runaway youth. *American Journal of Orthopsychiatry, 59*(2), 208–214.

Shinohara, M., and Jenkins, R. L. 1967. MMPI study of three types of delinquents. *Journal of Clinical Psychology, 23*(2), 156–163.

Smith, P., Bohnstedt, M., and Tompkins, T. 1979. Juvenile diversion evaluation: Report of an experimental study. In D. A. Henry (Ed.) *Pretrial services annual journal,* 118–140. Sacramento: California Department of the Youth Authority.

Sorenson, J. L. 1978. Outcome evaluation of a referral system for juvenile offenders. *American Journal of Community Psychology, 6*(4), 381–388.

Speck, N. B., Ginther, D. W., and Helton, J. R. 1988. *Adolescence, 23*(92), 881–888.

Spergel, I. A., Lynch, J. P., Reamer, F. G., and Korbelik, J. 1982. Response of organization and community to a deinstitutionalization strategy. *Crime and Delinquency, 28*(3), 426–449.

Spillane-Grieco, E. 1984. Characteristics of a helpful relationship: A study of empathic understanding and positive regard between runaways and their parents. *Adolescence, 19*(73), 63–75.

Stollery, P. L. 1977. Searching for the magic answer to juvenile delinquency. *Federal Probation* (December), 28–33.

Stratton, J. G. 1975. Effects of crisis intervention counseling on predelinquent and misdemeanor juvenile offenders. *Juvenile Justice, 26*(4), 7–18.

Sundeen, R. A. 1974. Police professionalization and community attachments and diversion of juveniles. *Criminology, 11*(4), 570–580.

Teilmann, K. S., and Landry, P. H. 1981. Gender bias in juvenile justice. *Journal of Research in Crime and Delinquency, 18*(1), 47–80.

Teitelbaum, L. E. 1983. Juvenile status offenders. In S. Kadish (Ed.), *Encyclopedia of Crime and Justice,* Vol. 3. New York: Free Press. pp. 983–991.

Thomson, D., and Treger, H. 1973. Police-social work cooperation and the overburden of the juvenile court. *Police Law Quarterly, 3*(1), 28–39.

Tsubouchi, K., and Jenkins, R. L. 1969. Three types of delinquents: Their performance on the MMPI and PCR. *Journal of Clinical Psychology, 25*(4), 353–358.

U.S. Department of Health and Human Services, Office of Human Development. 1980. *Annual report on the status and accomplishments of runaway youth programs.* Washington, D.C.: Youth Development Bureau.

U.S. Department of Health and Human Services, Office of Human Development Services, Administration for Children, Youth and Families. 1985. *Runaway and homeless youth: FY 1985 annual report to the Congress.* Washington, D.C.: U.S. Department of Health and Human Services.

U.S. Department of Health and Human Services, Region X Office of the Inspector General. 1983. *Runaway and homeless youth: National program inspection.* Washington, D.C.

U.S. General Accounting Office. 1983. *Federally supported centers provide needed services for runaway and homeless youths.* Washington, D.C.: U.S. General Accounting Office.

Van der Ploeg, J. D. 1989. Homelessness: A multidimensional problem. *Children and Youth Services Review, 11*(1), 45–56.

Warheit, G. J., et al. 1984. Selecting the needs assessment approach. In F. M. Cox, et al. (Eds.), *Tactics and techniques of community practice,* 2d ed. Itasca: F. E. Peacock.

Wells, M., and Sandhu, H. 1986. The juvenile runaway: A historical perspective. *Free Inquiry in Creative Sociology, 14*(2), 143–147.

Whittaker, J. K., Pecora, P. J. 1981. The social "R & D" paradigm in child and youth services: Building knowledge convivially. *Children and Youth Services Review, 3,* 305–317.

Williams, K. L. 1982. Attitudes toward violations and violative conduct among adolescents. Doctoral dissertation, State University of New York at Stony Brook.

Wolk, S., and Brandon, J. 1977. Runaway adolescents' perceptions of parents and self. *Adolescence, 12*(46), 175–187.

Woodside, M. 1980. Homeless youth: The saga of "pushouts" and "throwaways" in America. In U.S. Senate, *Report of the Subcommittee on the Constitution of the Committee on the Judiciary.* 96th Congress, 2nd Session. Washington, D.C.: United States Government Printing Office.

Young, T. M., and Pappenfort, D. M. 1977. *Secure dentition of juveniles and alternatives to its use: National Evaluation Program, phase one, summary report.* Washington, D.C.: National Institute of Law Enforcement and Criminal Justice (U.S. Department of Justice/LEAA).

Zabczynska, E. 1977. A longitudinal study of development of juvenile delinquency. *Polish Psychological Bulletin, 8*(4), 239–245.

Zatz, Julie. 1982. Problems and issues in deinstitutionalization: Historical overview and current attitudes. In J. Handler and J. Zatz (Eds.), *Neither angels nor thieves: Studies in deinstitutionalization of status offenders.* Washington, D.C.: National Academy Press.

Zieman, G. L., and Benson, G. P. 1980. School perceptions of truant adolescent boys. *Behavioral Disorders, Programs, Trends, and Concerns of Children with Behavioral Problems, 5*(4), 212–222.

Index